My Yorkshire Life

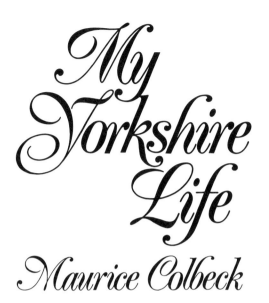

My Yorkshire Life

Maurice Colbeck

DALESMAN

First Published in Great Britain 1993 by
Dalesman Publishing Company Limited,
Stable Courtyard, Broughton Hall,
Skipton, North Yorkshire BD23 3AE
Text © 1993 **Maurice Colbeck**

British Library Cataloguing-in-Publication Data.
A catalogue record for this book is available from the British Library

To my family, past and present,
with affection and gratitude

ISBN **1 85568 066 1**
Typeset by **Lands Services**
Printed by **Biddles Limited**

Contents

ACKNOWLEDGEMENTS

INNUMERABLE people, consciously or otherwise, have contributed in various ways to the making of this book. I am grateful to them all, though many I am no longer able to thank personally. I think in particular of my late sister, Vera, who, by sharing her memories of our childhood, has enabled me to add much that might otherwise have been lost.

Through their books, two of my fellow Yorkshire journalists have awakened memories and filled gaps in my own knowledge. They are Derrick Boothroyd, author of *Nowt so Queer as Folk*, and Malcolm H. Haigh, whose *History of Batley 1800–1974* is invaluable to anyone writing about my quirky but in many ways admirable birthplace. I am also indebted to Margaret Fox's reminiscences, and to the publishers of the *Yorkshire Post*, *Yorkshire Life* and the *Batley News* for permission to use photographs or extracts from their pages.

I hope that any not mentioned above who have helped in any way (not least, as always, my wife, Brenda) will forgive the omission on the grounds of failing memory or sheer inadvertence.

1
Dickens and me

IT was the day of the 'school doctor's' periodic visit to a West Riding elementary school. Mothers sat on small desks pushed against a classroom wall as the doctor applied his stethoscope to their offsprings' chests. The Headmaster hovered in the wings, missing no opportunity to impress upon the medico that here was a school where hygiene was at least as important as long division.

Came the moment when we had to be weighed, and I mounted the scale immediately after a positive mountain of a boy, the very opposite of me in size and weight. Overcome by the importance of the occasion, the Head obviously felt that my diminutive stature reflected badly on the school. 'You look a funny chap, after so-and-so, don't you, Colbeck?' he accused, with unwonted heartiness. Resignedly. I agreed. Headmasters had to be humoured.

At home, with some disgust, I reported his remark to my mother. Her advice was typically spirited, if impractical. 'You should have said, "No sir, so-and-so's the funny chap, not me!"' It was an appealing idea, but headmasters, I knew, did not encourage repartee. Some of them indeed encouraged very little beyond a profound respect for their own strong right arms.

For some reason my mother had been absent from that particular inspection. There must have been a very pressing engagement elsewhere, or perhaps she'd reluctantly recognised that no matter what Mr Topliss thought about my size, I was now 'too big' to be accompanied by her on such occasions. In previous years she had been very much present, her smile composed in equal parts of maternal pride and sociability. And never was it brighter than when a visiting doctor complimented her on the protective qualities of my home-made flannel vest. Almost as if the other mothers had let him down, the Head said huffily, 'They're all taught needlework at school, doctor, they're all taught to do it.'

In those days, and not only in Yorkshire, a fat child was seen as a healthy child and Big was unquestionably Beautiful. Indeed, one of the earliest facts I ever learned was that Yorkshire was the biggest county in England. In itself, perhaps, that should not have weighed so heavily with a mere shrimp like me, but if any county had to be the biggest, then clearly, it must be Yorkshire.

Perhaps it was our historic supremacy in cricket, in the days when giants like Hutton, Sutcliffe and Leyland strode the earth, that encouraged us to see the Ridings as super-home to a super race; even if the benighted denizens of other counties thought our customs barbarous and our speech comic. Not that we felt any bitter scorn for such. Self-satisfied we may have been, but on the whole our common sense and native humour (then, as now, too often misunderstood), saved us from the worst excesses of arrogance.

We simply had no doubt that Yorkshire cloth, Yorkshire beer, the Yorkshire countryside and above all, Yorkshire folk were best. During a life-time lived largely in Yorkshire and half a lifetime spent editing a Yorkshire magazine, I have had countless opportunities to put these claims to the test – especially concerning the people. So just how do they measure up?

Certainly in their variety, the many I have known reflect the extensive territory that produced them. They include Dalesmen like Kit Calvert, Wensleydale personified, with his battered trilby, his weathered face, stumpy clay pipe and famous second-hand bookshop. Kit, your archetypal man of parts, saved his beloved Wensleydale cheese industry from extinction after the war while his other hand, so to speak, was translating the New Testament into Wensleydale dialect.

I remember, too, artists like Castleford-born Henry Moore and water-colourist Fred Lawson of Castle Bolton. At Scarborough, another Fred, the great Delius himself, seemed almost present in person as I talked with his selfless amanuensis, Eric Fenby, in a room containing the maestro's grand piano and his old wind-up gramophone. There was the tragic deaf and blind poet R.C. Scriven, whose determination to follow his calling cost him a private crucifixion. There were home-grown writers like J.B. Priestley, Phyllis Bentley, Stan Barstow, John Braine and William Holt of Todmorden, who travelled Europe on the white horse, Trigger, that he rescued from a rag and bone man's cart. And I remember, too, theatre folk like Ian Carmichael and Sonia Dresdel, the comedians Albert Modley and Harry Worth, a trio of archbishops and other assorted clerics of all persuasions.

And for me, an ex-elementary school boy and former mill lad, there was also the sudden confrontation with a breed of Yorkshiremen I had never encountered before – the county's landed gentry and aristocracy. Not that I found them particularly strange or intimidating: it was the reactions of others to what some called my 'hobnobbing' with the toffs that amused, irritated and puzzled me. When I wrote in *Yorkshire Life* about 'Lunch with Lord Harewood', for instance, it was because his background, such worlds apart from mine, and way of life aroused my curiosity and presumably that of my readers, too – not because the encounter made me feel 'one up'. I found it just as puzzling when a member of our board of directors saw that interview as something of a coup that would gain me, as he said, admission to every home in Yorkshire. I knew it wouldn't, and had he been a Yorkshireman, he would have known it too.

Social climbing had never formed any part of my family's thinking. Far from it. The cardinal sin in the eyes of people like us was to curry favour or suck up in any way to our 'superiors' – not that we were conscious of having any, be they headmasters, parsons or the foreman. The poor man's indestructible treasure in our view was his self-respect. The people I knew as a boy were often magnificent in their courage and their uncomplaining cheerfulness. But oh, what unrewarding jobs they had to do, what boredom they endured and how little was waiting for them at the end of all their toil! I made up my mind that, somehow, it was going to be different for me.

'YOU ought to be a writer when you grow up,' said Hermon Hall after marking another of my blot-stained 'compositions'. 'But write thrillers,' he would add companionably. 'I like thrillers.' And I liked Hermon. We all did, partly because he seemed incredibly old (he often reminded me that he had taught my father), and also because of his jokes and the fact that he never lost his temper.

Those jokes were rarely hilarious, but a joke was much more than a joke when a teacher told it. Our already well developed survival instincts told us that a joking teacher was a manageable teacher. All you had to do to relieve tedium, postpone work and ensure sir's good temper was laugh in the right places.

Being of a literary turn, Hermon often based his jokes on words – for instance, the little boy who, taken to the seaside, demanded to see 'the Tistherin'. In church he had heard in a psalm or lesson a phrase about 'the sea and all that is therein', so when, having got to Scarborough, he beheld the ocean, he demanded also to see... but you've got the point, as did the class, who spared no effort to demonstrate the fact by their vociferous mirth.

On the classroom wall of Standard VI hung a lithograph of Charles Dickens and from time to time Hermon would tell us, a little enviously perhaps, about the great novelist and how he used to be a newspaper reporter. Perhaps Hermon himself had hankered after a journalistic career – he certainly seemed cast in a different mould from most of the teachers I knew.

One day he instructed us to write out and then read aloud our favourite jokes. It was an opportunity one of the more daring spirits found irresistible. His joke, which he had already privily divulged to his 'mates', was read out with much spluttering of suppressed laughter. It was the sort of story that no-one would have dared to read out to any teacher but Hermon. I did not entirely comprehend it, but I knew it was 'mucky' and I quaked for its perpetrator.

I was shocked when Hermon laughed as loud as anyone. It was a joke I would never have dared to tell at home, though nowadays I doubt if a teacher would blench even to find it in an essay. Then, suddenly remembering his dignity, Hermon became propriety itself as he solemnly told the joker, 'Yours was a very rude joke, Jack. If I find anyone writing rude jokes I shall give him a good hiding.' And that was the funniest joke of the day, because Hermon would no more have given a lad a good hiding than he could have knocked out world heavyweight champion Carnera.

Hermon was a quietly powerful influence and remains a vivid memory, but I find it hard to recall him doing much formal teaching. If he was not joking or telling us about Dickens, Jules Verne or John Buchan, he was reminiscing. He seemed to know everybody and their fathers, sometimes their grandfathers. My own Grandad Colbeck, he used to tell the class, had been 'the finest tenor in the Heavy Woollen District. I remember him singing "Ev'ry valley shall be exalted", from Handel's *Messiah*, in Leeds Town Hall.' The implication underlying this proof of excellence seemed to be that you could forget all about less prestigious auditoria such as La Scala, Milan.

I wasn't sure whether I enjoyed or resented these revelations. Probably I was no more impressed by them than the rest of the class. I have never been more than mildly curious about my forebears. My son, the self-appointed family genealogist, says my great-grandfather married the daughter of a prominent mill-owner, but that apparently had precious little effect on the fortunes of his heirs and successors.

They seem to have been a rather mixed bag, lively, intelligent, enterprising but never blessed (or cursed) with too much success. When he wasn't singing Handel, my Grandad Colbeck was a confectioner locally renowned for his teacakes. No matter what their shortcomings, my recent ancestors at least shared in the musical heritage of the West Riding, which was as potent an influence for us as theirs is for the Welsh (though characteristically we Yorkshire folk didn't 'make such a song about it'!). For years a broken 'cello, once played by my maternal grandfather, stood in a corner of a bedroom in our little house in Batley.

By today's standards, all my grandparents died rather young. I can remember more than once being lifted up to look at waxen-faced forebears in their coffins, while surviving aunts and uncles remarked how 'peaceful' or 'beautiful' they looked, or described how, in their last moments, some had been cheered on their way by visions of heavenly bliss.

Perhaps because death was such an ever-present fact of life, the young were not shielded from the sight of it. I was probably about eleven, still too young for Hermon's class, when my little cousin Malcolm, not yet four years old, was knocked down and killed by a lorry while returning home from an errand. The tragedy was made all the more harrowing by the fact that shortly before he was born, his parents had lost an eight-year-old daughter, Joan, in a similar accident.

The *Batley News* reported: 'Tragedy, for the second time in four years, has bereaved and now left childless, the home of Mr and Mrs Walter Henry Colbeck. Mr Colbeck, a carpet weaver at Messrs Firth's mill, Heckmondwike, and his wife and a number of relatives were greatly distressed when a *News* reporter called to sympathise with them on Wednesday. The loss of little Malcolm has left the parents prostrate with grief.

'Mr Akeroyd (the undertaker) told our reporter that Malcolm was "a real wick little chap. He would dart here, there and everywhere, just like a shot from a gun," he said. "I told him many a time to be careful and to look up and down the road before crossing it."'

It was my first experience of personal tragedy. The sympathetic anguish felt by all the close family, especially my mother, was painful to see, but because we were not long out of the Victorian age it was still possible to soften the impact of death with ritual and sentiment. And so, along with three other male cousins of Malcolm, all aged less than twelve, I was chosen to serve as a coffin bearer at his funeral in St Peter's churchyard, Birstall. I can only suppose that this was at the request of Auntie Nelly, Malcolm's mother.

It was a bitter snowy day in the mid-1930s when the mourners fore-gathered in the usual way at Nelly and Walter's small stone terrace house. I remember still the sight of my usually talkative, ebullient uncle sobbing with his head on his wife's ample shoulder as they sat on hard upright chairs in the 'living room' to receive the mourners.

After the novelty of a taxi ride to the churchyard, we four small boys carried our smaller cousin to his grave. Auntie Nelly, following the teachings of her sect, did not expect to meet her children in the hereafter, it was said, because according to their doctrine, neither Joan nor Malcolm had been old enough for baptism when they died. The rest of the family, committed to more orthodox beliefs, were privately astonished by Nelly and Walter's ability to accept so final a separation from both their children.

The ceremony over, we were taken to a café in Birstall for that traditional Yorkshire funeral rite, 'the tea'. I don't recall that we buried little Malcolm 'with ham'. Uncle Walter could hardly have afforded that. He seemed to move from job to job, now and then trying his hand at shopkeeping but never with much success. Usually he was cheerful and talkative, perhaps a bit 'brussen', as such confident characters were called in the West Riding.

This dialect word was presumably derived from 'bursting' – with one's own opinions and self-importance of course. But he was far from brussen that day, though he tried to be cheerful as he thanked his son's four young pall-bearers and told us to make a good tea. I hope he forgave us our irrepressibly boyish high spirits, remembering we were too young to wonder how he felt when he thought of his own small boy alone in the cold churchyard.

My father, Walter's brother, was as far from being 'brussen' as a man could be. He was one of four brothers, all of whom served in the army during the First World War. One of them, Ernest, was commissioned. One day, he and one brother – was it Willie or Walter? – met somewhere in France. For a lark, they swapped uniforms and had their photographs taken in reversed roles to send home and bewilder their mother. The 'officer' sat grandly in the studio chair while the 'private' stood humbly alongside, but despite the solemn expression on each face, she would have had no difficulty recognising which son was which.

After his years in the trenches with the York and Lancaster Regiment, my father was probably grateful, like so many other survivors, just to be alive and able to put up with drudgery in the pit or the mill; happy enough to be conducting the chapel choir or building crystal sets when wireless was still a marvellous novelty; or dreamily playing tunes he would spontaneously compose at the little American organ in our single downstairs room. A lifelong abstainer from alcohol, he had no wish to spend his evenings in pubs or clubs and he was always willing to help me with my hobbies or my sums, a hopeless task, the latter, which could reduce him to helpless laughter at my ineptitude.

If he had ever known ambition it must have died on the Western Front, yet he did what he could to foster mine, while hardly expecting them to be realised. Fired, perhaps, by Hermon's advice that I should be 'a writer' and intrigued by his tales of Dickens, I had begun churning out unsaleable stories, articles and poems on a second-hand Royal Barlock typewriter for which my father forked out a hard-earned thirty shillings.

Possibly at my mother's prompting, he paid the instalments for me on a correspondence course with the Bennett College, Sheffield, whose advertisements bore a portrait of its principal over a caption reading 'Let me be your father'. There was an impressive picture of the college buildings and an equally impressive list of subjects spanning the alphabet, it seemed, from Accountancy to Zoology.

I felt no need of a father in Mr Bennett, but his prospectus dazzled me with promises of the success awaiting me once I had mastered the art of the short story. Diligently I sent off my exercises and eagerly awaited their return, liberally embellished with my tutor's red ink. The comments were encouraging but also full of common sense, despite what cynics were apt to tell me about correspondence schools.

Meanwhile I studied the lives of real writers. Perhaps, someday, I might write my own. But it seemed unlikely. I'd never heard of a writer from Batley.

2

The town where
I was born

HIDDEN somewhere in the lower half of Yorkshire, south of the
pastel-green fields and white shining limestone of the Dales, west
of the coast of Holderness and north of the Yorkshire coalfield,
you will find Batley.

That is, if you are looking for it, which to be honest, few do. From Surrey
and Kent, Yokohama and Minnesota they come in their thousands looking
for Brontë-haunted Haworth, only a score of miles north-west of Batley
as the crow flies. By the way, in the unlikely event that you ever do
seek Batley, you can estimate your proximity to the place by whether or
not the said crow flies backwards, which according to the local tradition
of neighbouring towns, birds do in Batley, but only 'to keep the muck
out o' their eyes'.

There's much less muck about these days, but the natives do still sometimes talk like that in Batley, mixing old Norse terms like 'fettle' with
Anglo-Saxon and eschewing the latest outrages inflicted on the language
by television, Americans and lah-di-dah southerners. Consequently, the
natives are all too often regarded as barbarians by any who stumble
inadvertently on this steep, stony world, as individualistic and tribal as
a village in the Welsh valleys.

Batley's pantheon includes deities like Joseph Priestley, the discoverer
of oxygen, whose birthplace within the former borough is marked by a
plaque, and Benjamin Law, the inventor of cloth woven from re-cycled
rags. Ben, perhaps, because he was for most of his life a Batley man, had
the sheer nerve, or lack of sense, to christen his creation 'shoddy'. (He was,
in fact, born at Gomersal, much closer to Batley than Haworth, but still
well known to Brontë-botherers for its Red House, which appears in
Shirley as 'Briarmain'.) Perhaps he foresaw the eventual confinement of
sheep to the moors and dales – and as befitted a Batley man – reasoned

thus: 'Yer mak' cloth fra' wool. Wool comes fra' sheep. Noa sheep, noa wool. Noa wool, noa cloth. Noa cloth, noa brass!' Since such a situation was clearly unacceptable, the fluffy stuff that keeps sheep warm appeared to be essential to life in Batley.

Unless, of course, you could use summat else. Why not, reasoned Benjamin (and here the true Batley genius manifests itself), why not make use of the wool that other folk had thrown away? In other words, the wool from old clothes? There is a legend explaining precisely how and where Ben had his brainwave: it is worth re-telling since it demonstrates the traditional impact of the far-from-backward Batley man on the 'superior' metropolis.

Benjamin was a clothier (as self-employed weavers used to be called) with a small-holding in the same Batley that his own success would change from semi-rural village to what a certain visiting southerner was later to describe as a 'vision of hell'. On St Bartholomew's Day, 1807, Ben was in London for the annual wool fair. In a Cheapside saddler's shop he was intrigued by the soft and cheap material used to stuff saddles. It was, he learned (no doubt by dint of subtle questioning), made from torn-up woollens. In other words, rags. 'Eureka,' Ben cried (or would have, if he'd had a classical education). Somehow, he just knew that the old, threadbare, worn-out stuff he was handling so knowledgeably could be transformed into summat that could be turned into brass!

But this was only the beginning. There was a vast distance to travel before this uninspiring material, even with the addition of a quantity of virgin wool, could be woven into anything like woollen cloth of marketable quality. Ben Law obtained some woollen rags, had them shredded as finely as possible, then spun them into thread from which he wove a few pieces of cloth. These he dyed in the hope of hiding their imperfections, but despite his best efforts he was far from pleased with the result. And this is where Benny Parr enters the story.

Before I had the slightest notion who Benny Parr might have been I knew his name. Or, more precisely, I knew the name of Benny Parr Wood. It ran along the banks of a stream at the bottom of a hilly area called Howley, on which stood the ruin of Howley Hall.

'Up Howley' was our local adventure playground when I was a lad, just as it was a playground for bigger, better-off, posher folk who frequented the golf club there. Even in my earliest youth there was very little left of Howley Hall, completed in 1590 for Lord Savile (to one of whose successors I was later to pay the ground-rent for the house where I still live in Batley). All that remained of Howley Hall in my boyhood were a few broken-down walls and gaping mouths of exposed cellars (dungeons, we called them, with utter certainty), as we fearlessly explored them in defiance of parental prohibitions. Long before I played there, my hero and favourite uncle, Frederick by name, who lived not far from Howley, had roamed those hills himself. One day he found a cannon ball which many years later he allowed me, wonderingly, to handle.

I knew, from a cork model in our local museum, that in the days of its grandeur, Howley Hall had been a magnificent structure with a flat roof on which visitors could actually play football! In 1643 one of my later heroes, Cromwell's patrician General Fairfax, held the house under siege. With Uncle Frederick's cannon ball in my hand I could hear and see in imagination the thunder and flash of cannon as Howley Hall, to quote Florrie Ford's song, became 'one of the ruins that Cromwell knocked abaht a bit'. The cannon ball might indeed have dated from Fairfax's siege, though it was not he who lowered it in its pride but the Earl of Cardigan, its owner in 1730, who apparently found it too expensive to maintain.

Come with me now a few rungs down the social ladder, back to Benny Parr, for Benny, too, played his part in the invention of shoddy cloth. His involvement, indeed, won a rather quirky fame for this man who might otherwise have been soon forgotten: for years ago, in London of all places, I met a venerable free-lance journalist who wrote for *The Waste Trade World*, or some such journal, under the aptest possible pseudonym of 'Benny Parr', the name of the man who had a part-share in the miracle of turning woollen rags into brass.

The original Benny Parr was, in fact, Benjamin Law's brother-in-law. He, too, was a clothier, but one with a turn for engineering, and therefore well equipped to produce a rag-grinding machine that would solve Ben Law's problem. The first results were promising, but still not immediately satisfactory, so, doubtless with due reluctance, a machine-maker in nearby Ossett was consulted. With his assistance, the process was improved until, in about 1813, after years of secret experiment, Benjamin Law's invention of shoddy cloth became public knowledge. Such was the horror (and possibly jealous rage) of more orthodox manufacturers that some of them couldn't bear the name 'shoddy', so they called the infernal new stuff 'made wool'. One of them, though anxious to profit by weaving it himself, would allow it to be delivered to his mill only at dead of night.

Law and Parr leased Howley Low Mill (probably the place I was chased away from as a lad, for throwing stones over the mill and into the dam). And there, besides making their own cloth, they conjured up new 'devils', as the rag-grinding machines were called, to meet the growing demand for raw shoddy from other manufacturers. In the churchyard of Batley's 15th century parish church of All Saints you may find a gravestone on which worn lettering tells the story of Benjamin Law, 'who died February 21st, 1837 . . . He was the inventor and first manufacturer of shoddy cloth and his best monument is the prosperity of the town where he resided, which has been raised from a mere hamlet to an important manufacturing town'.

Few would call Batley important today. You may blame the advent of man-made fibres, cheap foreign competition, failure by government or the effects of war, but the town's industrial decline was certainly not the fault of the bewildered local population. All too few of them, despite their reputation for skill and hard work, have been absorbed into the multitude of new industries which have moved in to fill part of the gap left by textiles. As Benjamin Law himself might have put it: *Sic transit gloria shoddy.*

As a native of Batley myself I find it not surprising, but strangely satisfying, that my own life was influenced – at least for a short time – by Benjamin Law. And so, indeed, was my father's.

AT the mill where Dad worked they had a fuddle in honour of my birth on 21 September 1925. A fuddle, let me explain, had nothing to do with being 'fuddled' – certainly in this case, for Dad was a teetotaller and anyway, the mill management would have tolerated nothing stronger than tea. No, a West Riding fuddle was a kind of celebratory shop-floor picnic to which all participants contributed – and probably shared – items of food. No doubt the main contributor was Dad.

I can imagine the warm-hearted, congratulatory banter as he and his workmates unpacked and pooled their offerings during a break in their machine-dominated toil, when voices echoed almost eerily in the sudden silence. 'Let's see, this is thi second bairn, in't it, Norman? An' a lad, this time. 'Ow many more do yer reckon there'll be?' And I can see Dad, friendly, but by nature non-committal on such a private matter, smile and shake his head before turning the conversation into more general channels: 'Onnyroad,' he perhaps speculated, 'Ah reckon he'll 'ave a better time of it nor we've 'ad.'

Dad was impressed by H. G. Wells and believed in progress, but so did the great majority then. No-one ever expressed mournful doubts as to whether the world they lived in was a fit place to be inhabited by yet more children. The War to end War had just been fought and – as nobody then doubted – won. There was no Bomb to cast its apocalyptic shadow over the future. Even Hitler was unheard of. True, many of the men who had put paid to Kaiser Bill were now blinded, crippled or on the dole. But surely the future would be bright.

I am not aware that they had a fuddle at the Maternity Home about a quarter of a mile away, when I first entered the world. I am sure there were plenty of visitors to smile at the new arrival and speculate as to which of his forebears he 'took after' – whether he was 'a Poole or a Colbeck' – and wasn't it nice to have a boy this time, though every woman should be glad to have a daughter, of course. 'Yer son is yer son till he gets a wife, but yer daughter's yer daughter all 'er life,' they would pronounce, sagely, these ladies in their funny high hats, which a few years later were my first indication of the troublesome but interesting fact that the world contained two sexes.

'If 'e turns out as well as yer first, you'll 'ave nowt to complain about,' they almost certainly said, able to speak freely in the absence of that 'first', who was still blissfully unaware that she had a brother. Temporarily billeted on relations in a rural corner of the district, my sister Vera never forgot that childhood heaven where, as the youngest in the house and fair game for spoiling, she went to bed when she felt like it, ate what, and how much or little she wanted and was not debarred by mere youth from having preferences. Things were a little stricter at our house.

The birthplace of thousands of my fellow townsfolk, the Maternity Home could truthfully be said to embody the very essence of the town, and not just because it was built of soot-black stone and fronted by a dank, tree-shadowed garden on the road which ran along the oft-flooded, mill-lined valley-bottom route linking Batley with Bradford.

To start with, the Maternity Home was bought as Rock House by no less than 'Batley's greatest son', Theodore C. Taylor, in 1919. He presented it to the town three years before I was born, as a memorial to his wife and daughter. Theodore, who no doubt felt that the title Batley bestowed upon him was thoroughly merited, was an 'old boy' of the town's venerable Grammar School. He came of a family which built the first five-storeyed mill in Batley. His uncle Thomas, one of the architects of the Taylor kingdom, had been so delighted with its sky-scraping chimney that he had triumphantly dangled his legs from its parapet. Theodore, who eventually and inevitably inherited this woollen world, was woven of less frivolous stuff. Before he was thirty he had opened Batley's first weaving school (the forerunner of its Technical College); but what most amazed Batley and set 'T.C.' apart from all other mill-owners was the profit-sharing scheme he instituted.

If you'd spent your working life at Taylors', where bonuses were paid as shares in the company, publication of your will in the *Batley News* or *Reporter* would be eagerly awaited, for there could be no doubt that you'd left a bob or two. Taylors' 'divi' was declared at each annual meeting in the works canteen. At this momentous event, even after he had passed his century (he lived to be 102), Theodore would hold forth to a rapt audience on the state of trade and of the world and on the blessings consequent on sober, industrious and God-fearing lives like his.

'Work hard and you will get on . . . Keep trying and you'll succeed,' he would assure students as he presented them with their prizes won at the Technical College. He may not have made it sound easy, but he managed to make it sound certain. Whether he ever reflected that he had been given rather a good start in life, who can say? Meanwhile, families like ours made the best of things, only too thankful – if we were old enough to think about such things – that our fathers had jobs of any sort. As for prospects or ambitions, as Shaw's immortal dustman said of morals, we couldn't afford 'em.

3
Wool and worship

I N the Batley of my boyhood, life for most folk revolved around the mill, the pub (or club) or the chapel. In our case it was the chapel. We belonged to a small denomination, better known in Lancashire than in Yorkshire, called the Independent Methodists. Methodists of the more orthodox variety there were in plenty. Their Ebenezers, Bethels and Mount Tabors bore witness in almost every street to their scriptural orthodoxy. Every other person you met was a Methodist and in theory at least, Methodism was the creed of the shoddy manufacturers. So much so that the splendid Zion chapel on Commercial Street was popularly known as 't' Shoddy Temple'.

'There were more business done on t' Zion steps on a Sunday morning,' it was said, 'than in t'Bradford Wool Exchange.' But Methodist industrialists, unlike their Quaker counterparts, were not noticeably given to worshipping in silence. And if they were not actually punctuating the sermon with 'Hallelujahs' or 'Amens', some were certainly whole-hearted enough in their hymn-singing.

Charlie Robinson was such a one, though I knew of him only as a legend. The dales and moors had their giants, such as Rombald and Wade. We had Charlie. His chapel-going, it seemed, did nothing to reduce his ruthlessness as an employer. On the contrary, if Charlie were seen 'roarin' (weeping) with religious fervour in chapel on Sunday, his workers would tremble. They knew all too well that come Monday morning he would be all the more tyrannical to make up for it. Perhaps guilt played a part in these displays. Certainly it may have motivated the secret acts of charity which were so lauded in the obituaries printed on his death in 1929. I was four years old then, and living in a halcyon state untroubled by harsh employers or even bad-tempered teachers. I had yet to wince under the spur of my first editor, the redoubtable Rayner Roberts, who was himself to tell me one of the best-known tales about Charlie.

It concerned the traveller (sales representative) who had called for years at Charlie's office, without once announcing the purpose of his visit. On every occasion the conversation went like this:

'Owt?' enquired the traveller.

'Nowt,' replied Charlie.

'Mornin',' said the traveller.

'Mornin',' replied Charlie.

Stories about him were legion. One my father told me was based on Charlie's propensity to dismiss any man he found idling, apparently on the principle: 'If it doesn't move, sack it'. He would even 'sack' employees sent with messages from other factories if he found them waiting in the mill-yard. Once, having sacked a young lad he suspected of idling, he was told: 'Aye, tha can seck me, Mr Robi'son, but tha can't seck mi fayther!'

Such fighting talk incensed Charlie to fever pitch. 'Ah'll show thi if Ah can seck him,' he roared. 'Which department does he work in?' 'None o' thine,' said the lad. ''E's a foreman at Taylor's.' One version of the story has Charlie offering the lad a job in tribute to his ready wit, but that may well be apocryphal, for characters like Charlie attract legend on legend as surely as honey attracts flies.

Manufacturing Methodists such as Charlie may have been fervent in prayer in the chapel on Sundays, but we doubted if they could compete with us Independent Methodists when it came to musical fervour. After all, we were descended from a sect nicknamed 'The Singing Quakers', to distinguish them from the original Quakers who eschewed hymn-singing as mere formality.

I believe that upon occasion they do burst into song nowadays, just as they do many other generally acceptable things besides providing paternal-istically for their employees in the manner of that great Yorkshire phil-anthropist the Congregationalist Sir Titus Salt. On the banks of the River Aire at Shipley, he built not only the biggest mill in the world but a 'model village' with all the amenities deemed necessary by the Victorians for cleanliness and godliness – churches, schools, washrooms and laundries – but no pubs or pawn shops.

Batley may not have produced Sir Titus, but it had perhaps gone one better by producing the profit-sharing mill-owner Theodore Taylor, whom we met in the last chapter. Theodore, himself a Congregationalist, was at least as famous in his day and generation as Salt. The great-grandson of a handloom weaver, Abraham Taylor, Theodore was head of a company which owned several mills in Batley and at one time employed 1,500 people. He gained the reputation of a hard taskmaster who had the power to terrify his departmental heads, especially one who was apparently prepared to miss a departmental meeting, just because he had planned instead to visit Doncaster on St Leger Day. Not, you understand, to back horses, as the poor man squirmingly protested when challenged by the chairman, but purely 'for the spectacle'. The truth may well have been, as my old colleague Derrick Boothroyd suggests in his delightful book *Nowt So Queer as Folk*, that Theodore, having learned of his minion's intention, had deliberately arranged a meeting for Leger Day to engineer a show-down.

An exacting employer he certainly was, but in his own way a generous one. His hundredth birthday was celebrated with a trip to Blackpool by special train for every one of his workers, during which the centenarian mill-owner was photographed accompanying some of his girl workers as they danced the palais glide in the Winter Gardens ballroom.

Such frivolous activity, however, was far from his normal mode of life. As he was driven to the mill in his Daimler on three days a week from his home at Grassington in Wharfedale, he would pass the time reading aloud from the hymn book. He made no secret of the religious convictions which had led him to introduce profit-sharing, undeterred by the fact that this resulted in a family dispute. But though he was a Nonconformist in the classic mould, he was one almost by accident: he might easily have remained the Anglican he was born if effluent from the dyehouse of Taylor's Blakeridge Mill, the biggest in Batley, had not flowed through the vicar's garden on its way to Batley Beck.

The vicar relished neither its smell nor its apparently repulsive colour. Despite the three Taylor brothers' claim that they had an ancient right on their side, the reverend gentleman insisted that they must either stop polluting the priestly precincts or pay for the privilege. The day came when Theodore's Uncle Tom stood in Batley parish church with the vicar's writ in his pocket. He never went there again and neither, so the story goes, did any other member of the Taylor clan.

Although one of my forebears was apparently enterprising enough to have married his particular boss's daughter (the boss being a Batley mill-owner), there were no Daimlers in my family and to the best of my knowledge, no member of our Independent Methodist congregation was ever a millionaire. The nearest we ever got to harbouring a celebrity was when the local baths manager, a refugee from Wigan who delighted us all by calling a bus a buzz, joined our congregation. I had a brief, eleven-year-old romance with his daughter, after which (though I doubt that it was a case of cause and effect) the baths manager left to return to Wigan or possibly even more exotic climes, and our brush with greatness was at an end.

The words of St Paul might be said to have applied as much to us as to the Corinthians, for not many of us were wise, not many of us were powerful and certainly none of us was of noble birth. The one thing that distinguished the staunchest adherents of our sect was unwavering dedication to its professed principles, which in theory at least included total abstinence from 'strong drink' and, by implication, from many other popular but supposedly sinful activities.

There were those amongst us who certainly seemed to have no fears that the occasional drink would imperil their souls. One such was Simon Sheard whose daughter Sally was a lifelong friend of my mother's and one of my adopted 'aunties'. Simon used to emphasise the rhythm of his favourite hymns by vigorously jingling his money in his pocket in time with the beat. When the hymn was officially ended, he would roar out the last stanza over again, dragging both organist and usually reluctant congregation with him.

In business as a market gardener Simon was said to frequent the Knottingley Wells Hotel near his garden. With Simon's grandson, Arthur, I used to catch water skaters and release newts in the little pond where Simon filled his watering cans until the gentle, if sometimes irascible, man got fed up of our chatter, sent us on our way and possibly retired to the Knottingley Wells for something to calm his nerves.

Doubtless many other supposed prohibitions were more honoured in the breach than the observance, but since that concerning 'strong drink' was usually the only one discussed, it was virtually impossible to discover what was allowed and what forbidden, much less what was actually done. And yet our ranks held many kindly and loving souls who were, I am sure, far less censorious of the failings of others than some of those who had less reticence about discussing them.

There was, for instance, 'Little Ernest', the tiny, invariably cheerful man whose legs were bent at the knees almost in the shape of a letter K. His mode of locomotion was possibly more painful to watch that it was for him to perform, but I doubt if he could have progressed very far without the white stick that supported him and also announced that he was almost blind. Cripples in those days were commonplace, due no doubt to generations of poor feeding, excessive working hours and generally bad conditions.

But it was often those most afflicted who seemed the happiest. As a mere shrimp myself, I was amazed to see how readily Little Ernest joined in the jokes about his low stature. His chief delight was the drum kit he would play at 'concerts'. I used to feel that his moment of glory should have come on the heady occasions when the choir, amazingly costumed, performed an 'opera', which was their generic title for productions of *A Waltz Dream* or one of the Gilbert and Sullivan creations. No Broadway production ever aroused more excitement in its participants. There was even an orchestra of two or three local musicians and a tympanist who would accompany our home-grown performers. But Little Ernest was not among them.

'Why isn't Little Ernest playin'? It isn't fair,' I protested. But the little knock-kneed man did not protest. Instead, as he sat with the children on the front row of the audience in the Sunday school, he would peer with myopic admiration at the drummer who, on great occasions such as this, had been given what was usually his place.

4

The hanged man

MRS TONG opened her eyes wide with horror as she and my mother met over the wall that divided our eleven front steps from her tiny garden.

Silently she mouthed the news that somebody – I didn't catch the name – had 'hanged hissen'. I wondered who he was and what exactly he had done and why it could not be spoken of openly. At five years old I thought I knew what 'hanging' meant: you hung pictures on the wall and clothes in the big wardrobe where my sister and I used to hide, but why, and where, would a man hang himself?

My mother listened dutifully to her neighbour, who, her story told, returned indoors. Until then I had remained silent: it was rather a crime to interrupt the mysterious communings of grown-ups – not that they were interesting enough, usually, to be worth the risk. But this man who had hanged himself . . . Now that I was free to talk at last, the questions bubbled from me like water from a long-dammed stream.

After my mother's brief explanation the story seemed even more amazing. The man, whoever he was, had 'hanged himself' in order to die. Why? Because he did not wish to live. I felt no stirrings of horror or compassion, only amazement that such things could be. I lost no sleep over him, whoever he was, shed no tears and as far as I know, acquired no complexes; yet the memory of that fleeting, microscopic episode has stayed with me for sixty years.

In the thirties, when I first became aware of the world, no one seemed to doubt that life was good – while recognising that for most folk it could and should have been a great deal better. Seven years before I was born, the most devastating war ever fought had ended. Thousands who had been called heroes while it lasted had now no job to justify their claim to man-hood, and many had survived the war only to perish in the peace. And yet life for the moderately lucky had a glow of happiness. At least it had for me, for school was still no more than something my sister prattled about when she wasn't dragooning me into silly games or otherwise exercising her ten-year-old big sister's authority. Still, if I did not suffer, the cat did, whether from being squashed mercilessly into her doll's pram or having its capacity to deal with gravity tested by being dropped from our elevated front door into the yard below – to the horror of the two old women, Mrs Norton and Mrs Hammond, who lived beneath us like troglodytes in spotless, one-roomed dwellings.

They relied on us for a great deal, and my mother, who loved old folk as much as she loved children, never failed them, even 'laying-out' Mrs Hammond when one morning she found her dead, or at least close to death. At first she and another neighbour tried to revive her by placing hot water bottles around her body. A little colour had come back to her cheeks, my mother reported later, but it was soon beyond doubt that life had fled.

So what, now, would become of Mrs Hammond's cat, a beautiful silver-grey animal, as 'ladylike' in her feline way as Mrs Hammond herself. I pleaded that we might take her, but was told the cat would never settle with anyone else. So a man from the top of the street, who kept ferrets and had a tawny lurcher dog called Mick, took the cat away in a sack. My soft-hearted mother shed a tear or two, but in those days, cats, no matter how refined, had not much status.

Yet most people, it seems to me in retrospect, were kind. I wandered at will in and out of the stone houses in our short, steep street, though generally, my mother preferred me to confine my socialising to the bottom end, where we lived. We were not consciously snobbish – perhaps no-one is – but at our end of the street we were . . . different. There were no 'rows', for instance, though from a distance we enjoyed watching those at the top. Among ourselves we preserved at least a facade of civility most of the time, the women smiling, sometimes mechanically, when they met in the street, the men grunting ''Ow do?' as they passed each other on the way home from work.

There were times, however, when we had no choice whether or not to visit the top of the street, because there, in the yard where we had our Guy Fawkes Night bonfire, stood a row of four or five brick-built water closets, each shared by two or three families whose womenfolk scrubbed them frenziedly turn and turn about until the scoured wood of the seats shone like snow.

Across the street from the yard lived the ferret man's family, of Irish extraction, comprising father, a man of few words, his plump and lively wife, a brood of small and pretty girls as red-haired as their mother, and the only boy of the family, Lawrence. How Lawrence and I became friends

I hardly remember, but I feel sure it had something to do with the alien glamour of their way of life, epitomised for me by the cage of ferrets in the tiny yard and by Mick, the lurcher dog, licking himself as he lay at insolent ease on the flagstones outside their terrace house.

I had never had a dog – or ferrets: only rabbits and guinea pigs and the young rook I found and tamed. I had no boxing gloves, either. I knew it would be useless to ask for them: my mother would have considered them rough and a bit common. I don't suppose she was favourably impressed, either, when I told her of the big photograph of Lawrence's dad in boxing kit hanging over the fireplace.

In the yard where the privies stood, Lawrence and I would spar for hours at a time. I can still feel the sudden agony as Lawrence's punch caught me off balance at the same instant as I tripped backwards over the edge of an iron manhole cover. As my bony bottom sharply connected with the unyielding metal, I realised for the first time, the incommunicability of pain. I had fallen a hundred times without feeling a pain like that, but I knew better than to mention it.

I've no doubt Lawrence's punches connected more often with me than mine did with him. I feel sure that though he tolerated me when his real friends were unavailable he hardly recognised me as a real part of his world. He, on the other hand, was real enough to me. Perhaps he answered a hunger for toughness awakened in me by my over-protected upbringing. I yearned to be tough. Tom Sawyer was my hero from the moment I saw him brought to enviable, glorious life on the screen by Jackie Coogan and, later, Jackie Cooper. I yearned to be what in Yorkshire was called 'a real lad', but the scales were weighted against me. I was expected to be a model of cleanliness and tidiness, an ideal which was doubtless attainable by any number of boys, but never, alas, by me.

When Lifebuoy, or some other soap company, instituted a 'Clean Hands Campaign' at our infants' school, I inevitably won a first-class certificate, though it was gained entirely by false pretences. If my mother had not religiously soaped my visible person daily after breakfast and lunch, ready for the inspections that followed at school, my reward would have probably taken a different and more painful form.

But if I took little pride in the virtue that is closest to godliness, she took pride enough for both of us in my 'Clean Hands' certificate – for a time at least. When, in one of her bouts of frustration, she removed it from the bedroom wall where she had pinned it among my pictures of ships and cowboys, she told me, sadly, that I had failed to 'live up to it'. I refrained from telling her how glad I was to see the back of it, and hoped she took my silence for remorse.

5
Albert Street

THEY don't build streets like Albert Street any more – but were such streets ever really 'built'? Rather, they grew, organically, like coral reefs or giant ant-hills on the remains of their predecessors. Albert Street presumably received its name sometime during the score of years when Prince Albert Francis Charles Augustus Emmanuel of Saxe-Coburg-Gotha was the idolised consort of Queen Victoria and, through her, a future influence on thousands yet unborn, including me.

Or perhaps a local builder named the street after his own son Albert. In either case, the influence, direct or indirect, came from the same source and I was equally unaware of it. Just as well. I would not have been pleased to learn that the street where I was raised owed anything to a reputedly German prince, one of the race my Dad had fought in the war.

Albert Street sloped up from Field Lane, which no longer had any dealings with a field. Its title was doubtless bestowed on the school before the intervening network of setted streets – Albion Street, Queen Street and Albert Street – was built. Field Lane remains, but Albert Street is no more. I dearly wish it could have been preserved for the amazement of future generations.

If you had to grow up in a street, you could have done far worse than choose Albert Street. With the eccentricities of its yards and ginnels and unlikely bits of garden and its unexpected social divisions, it was a world awaiting discovery, an adventure playground in itself. The very antithesis of the characterless modern housing estate, let alone a tower block of flats, its every house was different, though none more different than ours!

You reached our front door (there was no back door) by eleven steps divided by two landings into flights of three or four each. At one side the steps were bordered by a smooth-topped wall down which I would attempt to slide when out of sight of my mother. (At one time a wooden gate made by Dad was fixed midway up the steps to limit my wanderings and frequent tumbles down this Everest of painstakingly white-edged steps.) At the other side of the steps there were railings lined with wooden boxes painted green and planted with 'storshuns' as my mother called nasturtiums. Literally beneath our house on that side was a single-storey dwelling, one of a pair, opening on one of those inevitable yards, and each occupied by an old woman on whom my mother lavished much of her over-abundance of care.

Across the street was a paved yard with houses on one side. It seemed an ordinary rectangle until you reached what appeared to be the end, only to find that there it assumed an L-shape with an added quadrangle to accommodate not one, as you might have expected, but two houses. Perched five feet or so higher than this paved area, like a terrace in a rice paddy, was a green yard, almost a tiny common, where I was wont to dig holes with the 'pot 'ole shovel' my mother used to clear ash from the fireplace, and where I would start fires in the grass with pilfered matches.

Looking out on this green no-man's-land was a row of houses, each with its 'bit o' garden', one of which contained the guinea pig shed of Mr Johnson (as I must call him, having long ago forgotten his real name). He was a quiet, serious man who bred and showed the animals whose rosettes and certificates, won at this show and that, adorned the wooden walls of their dwelling. I bought my first pair of cavies from him and would stand beside him in his shed as, heavy-handedly, he would stroke the gleaming fur of his button-eyed charges. I wondered if they liked it. They appeared docile enough but it seemed on his part more of a grooming exercise than a demonstration of affection. With youthful brashness I cultivated his aquaintance and assimilated his knowledge, but never learned what he felt for his guinea pigs, or indeed about anything else.

It was different with Harley Pickard, who lived in the next street. Harley, slim, bespectacled and bushy-haired, whose name seemed ready-made for a Yorkshire novel, was a piano-tuner and reputedly 'not a well man'. That must have been why his patient, friendly wife went out to work while he stayed at home between piano-tuning jobs, wearing, I seem to remember, a white apron, to protect his suit from household chores.

It must have been Harley's canary which started our friendship. In the face of the burgeoning budgie boom of the time, the demure but tuneful canary had become something of a rarity. Harley's eyes sparkled with enthusiasm at my interest as, in a small back bedroom, he introduced me to what seemed another world. Here, more canaries were breeding; while in a larger cage, tiny birds with red markings suggesting that they had had their throats cut, flitted interminably from perch to perch. Indifferent to these hyper-active neighbours, in a glass tank liberally planted with flourishing green weed, swam a placid goldfish named Freddie.

I must have been a confident kid – at least with adults – to have made so many acquaintances, who, in retrospect at least, seem to have tolerated me with such equanimity. Am I wrong in thinking that people were kinder in those days? Children, on the whole, expected to be liked, and though the show-offs would be quickly cut down to size, cunning little ingratiators like me rarely outstayed their welcome.

Nowadays I might have been dubbed manipulative, but what child isn't? In an adult-dominated world children need all the advantages nature can give them. Not that great skill was needed to deal with most grown-ups, teachers included: I often marvelled at the gullibility of the average adult in dealing with the most transparent mendacity. Perhaps the fact that my upbringing had made me almost incapable of telling a downright lie enhanced my skill in subtler methods of deceit.

But in my earliest years I had no need to dissemble. Every door in the street seemed open to me, notably that of the Blamires. Within lived old Mr Blamires in patriarchal dignity with his wife and their middle-aged son Ben and daughter Mary Lizzie. Their tiny house was filled with Victorian bric-a-brac that, amazingly, I was free to play with. I can recall Mrs Blamires's smile easily even today, and the old dialect turns of phrase she used which I carried away in my head and pestered my mother to explain. The old couple were among her pets, though the old man did not always win favour. During some forgotten crisis in their family, my mother took the old man a meal, including the dumplings on whose lightness she so prided herself. It proved a sad mistake.

I recall her aggrieved expression as she returned to our house with the plate in her hand. Whatever could have happened? She was unable to with-hold the dreadful truth: instead of delicately teasing her fluffy creations apart with his fork, old Mr Blamires, in some mad frenzy of male brutality, had actually taken his knife to them! 'I could have smacked him,' she said. I believed her. It was one of those moments of revelation that survive the years. Your parents, believe it or not, are not always right: my sympathies were with Mr Blamires.

There were a brother and sister, George and Stella, who lived with their aged mother at the top of the street. Stella, dignified and refined, used to compliment my mother (much to my disgust) on 'your beautiful children' – the last thing I wanted to be called was beautiful. Stella seemed to belong to another world, as indeed, in another sense, did her brother. With his leggings, broad-brimmed hat and dashing moustache, George was like an empire builder as depicted in the ancient boys' magazine called *Chums*. And the resemblance was more than superficial, for George, as I later gathered, had spent some years in North America where he had made a living selling, among other things perhaps, sewing-machines to oil-rich Red Indians.

In retrospect it is the amazing variety of this rich mix of neighbours which most astonishes me about our little street, and the intricacies of their relationships with each other. Like recognized like, while the disparate elements barely seemed aware of each other's existence. Only the youngest could move freely across these boundaries, which no doubt explains my friendship with the Misses Calvert.

These two maiden ladies kept a tiny shop on Commercial Street, Batley's main shopping thoroughfare, selling artists' materials and little toys such as lead soldiers and small Victorian-style dolls which, to my eyes at least, they strangely resembled. If they made a living I can't imagine how. I suppose the shop had first belonged to the revered parent they called 'Fawther'. It was Fawther they talked about as I sat in their little house two or three doors from ours. He had been an artist and craftsman and they showed me with pride treasured examples of his pictures and wonderful work in marquetry.

The Misses Calvert lived half-way up our street, which seemed to change its character near the top. It was the upper street dwellers (with notable exceptions like George and Stella) who occasionally enlivened our days with their 'rows'. I can remember watching such events with great enjoyment as I sat at the top of the steps leading to our door. The altercations always began with verbal abuse which increased in intensity until words were no longer enough and the contestants would advance into the middle of the street and engage in hand-to-hand combat. These conflicts, usually caused by disagreements over children, rarely lasted long or caused real injury. They may well have relieved frustrations born of poverty and monotony. But for the most part, the street's inhabitants passed their days, if not quite in the Prayer Book's 'rest and quietness', at least in a state of co-operation and harmony.

'Top o' t' street' was not exactly out of bounds to me but I was never encouraged to go there. In any case I had little desire to. I knew that there I was an interloper, rather than one of Jinny's 'beautiful' children and thus fair game for spoiling. Generally speaking, the women who lived there eyed me coldly, having enough with their own plentiful kids and the overspill these attracted from the rougher elements of Albion Street and, beyond that, Queen Street, famous as the home territory of 'T'Edie Ann', at once the terror and the butt of the Field Lane neighbourhood kids.

I suppose she was originally christened Edith Ann, but in the local vernacular she had long been 'T'Edie Ann' and that was the name children chanted after her, from a safe distance, whenever they got the chance:

T'Edie Ann,
Tin can,
Copper kettle, brass pan.

That safe distance was considered very necessary, for 'T'Edie' had a dog and carried a dog whip which she reputedly thought nothing of using on the legs of her persecutors. As I remember her, she wore leggings and a coal-heaver's jacket and smoked a clay pipe. We never doubted that she was a woman but she was uncompromisingly, aggressively masculine; more of a man than the men, or some of them. I viewed her with a mixture of fear and fascination, but how did she see herself, I wondered, and what did she think of the world that found her so comic or so strange? Poor T'Edie Ann! Perhaps, as we would more readily recognise today, she had simply, sadly been born the wrong sex.

Margaret Fox, a local writer whose memories of bygone Batley characters are eagerly read, has found her public insatiable for recollections of T'Edie Ann. Having ventured to give a lecture without, for once, mentioning that strangely fascinating creature, she was followed to her car by disappointed 'T'Edie' fans demanding an explanation for such an incredible omission.

Margaret Fox's researches have in fact revealed a character much more complex than the one we feared or mocked as children, a woman desperate for affection but incapable of inspiring it, and, most poignant of all, perhaps, a lover of children who would peer through school windows, just to get a glimpse of them.

WHEN I explored Field Lane the other day in search of Albert Street, I found that not only had it vanished, but there seemed to be hardly a space it could have occupied. One side of Whitaker Street, which had run parallel with Albert Street, remained, containing the house where the 'bonesetter', Mr Lodge, had lived. But gone was the house to which, early in the war years, we had moved eager to enjoy the blessings of electricity instead of gas lighting and – supreme luxury – a fixed bath. Gone, too, was the patch of waste ground where we had erected our 'Anderson' air raid shelter and where my father had later made a garden to fill the hours thrust upon him by unwelcome early retirement.

Our new home had been opposite the Lodges' residence, palatial compared with ours, where Mr and Mrs Lodge lived with (I think) Mrs Lodge's aged father. They were devout friendly, warm and gently humorous, with none of the harshness a later age in its ignorance has wished upon such Nonconformist folk. When the aged parent lay dying, my mother told me, his voice could be heard during his last days as he made his peace with his Maker. 'It does you good to hear him,' said the innocent Mrs Lodge, apparently with no suspicion that her words might be uncharitably misconstrued.

She and my mother, who helped her with domestic tasks in their largish house, were great friends. My mother much admired Mr Lodge's manipulative skill, whose effects she could observe from our window when patients visited the Lodge residence and consulting rooms. Mrs Lodge, too, was greatly in awe of her husband's abilities, which, although he had studied under another practitioner, she attributed principally to 'a gift'.

'I think it's wonderful,' my mother would breathe as she recounted the improvement in the condition of a small child, born, apparently, with her feet reversed, but after several weeks of Mr Lodge's ministrations, able to run as freely as any other. This small, humble, friendly man was surely as much a healer in his way as two of his sons who became, I believe, respectively a doctor and a dentist. Another son was killed in action flying with the RAF, a grief my mother shared with his.

But the only children who ran about Whitaker Street on the day of my return visit were darker-skinned than any I had seen there in my early teens, though their accents were as obviously Yorkshire as mine. At the top of Whitaker Street, Field Lane School, where I went as an 'infant' of five, is now almost entirely populated by bright-eyed Pakistani children. A few years ago I found them in the care of a headmistress as unlike the Miss Terry I remembered from my Field Lane days as she could be.

She seemed perfectly at home in a role she tackled with understanding and imagination. Attractively wearing the Islamic woman's costume of scarf, tunic and trousers as a 'visual aid', she would give talks on the way she and her staff tried to establish and maintain a rapport with their pupils through a knowledge of their religion, customs and family life. When, for instance, a little Islamic girl covers her doll's face as it lies in a cot, it would be so easy to say, 'We don't cover babies' faces, do we?' Thus a child's mind could become confused simply because it had been forgotten that in Pakistan, if not in Yorkshire, mosquitoes are a problem.

The school remains, but the glorious mish-mash that was Albert Street in the days when a dark face was seen only on the occasional turbanned pedlar opening his case for my mother's hesitant inspection, might never have existed. Now there were new houses with gardens ready made (not improvised, like Dad's, with home-made fencing) and glowing with flowers whose size would have aroused his envy. Instead of the sooty atmosphere that pervaded that part of the town before 'clean air' had become a cliché, I recognised a scent I had never known until the Navy took me to distant, eastern climes. No mystery nowadays, the smell of curry.

Today, Batley, which once relied on the all-purpose Co-op Cafe for its businessmen's lunches or on its fish and chip shops, its pie and pea vendors and its sandwich-making bakeries for the sustenance of its toiling (or work-less) masses, has Chinese, Indian, even Italian restaurants; while every other pub seems to offer exotic lunchtime delights. ('Lasagne? What the 'ell's that?' they would have said in my teenage years. 'I like to be able to see what Ah'm eytin'.')

Those old-timers, would never have believed that Batley folk could have been persuaded to devour such stuff – and at such prices! Even if you had forewarned them of the sad diminution in the value of the pound, they would have been overwhelmed by the apparent evidence all around of barely believable affluence: that is, if the sight of two cars in the garage of a so-called 'working class' family had not persuaded them that they were living in a world of fantasy.

And what about our mosque? West Riding Methodists and Congregationalists long ago became accustomed to the acquisition of their forsaken temples by followers of the Prophet, but what, I ask again, about our mosque? The fact that we call it ours must indicate a certain pride of possession, but only in the sense that Batley is 'our' town. For the mosque can only properly belong to the faithful – and, of course, to Allah.

I have removed my shoes to enter the mosques and temples in Jerusalem, Cairo, Colombo and Samarkand, have stood in the mosque built around the rock where Abraham would have slain his son but for the restraining voice of God, but I know nothing more remarkable to one raised in the Batley of my youth than our mosque. Perhaps the kindness of its authorities in permitting friendly infidels to tour its sacred precincts on the opening day does tend to encourage a sense of ownership.

Its first appearance startled even Batley out of its accustomed phlegm. Most of our oldest inhabitants had probably seen nothing like it since watching *Beau Geste* at the Super Cinema when that temple of escapism was still standing. But as their astonished eyes traced the exotic outline of our mosque's minarets, they asked each other, 'Did yer ever see owt like it?' while slightly younger inhabitants, such as I, found themselves instantly transported back in time and east of Suez.

But Batley, when it goggles, goggles not for long. Soon we had ceased to marvel at the mirage of that graceful outline rising from the landscape of privet hedges, stone terrace houses, corner shops and St Andrew's parish church, unshaken by the presence of its new neighbour. Sadly, with familiarity came contempt. When, inevitably, some idiotic outrage of vandalism was committed, the people of the Prophet generously recognised that such acts did not represent the feelings of their saner neighbours, while the indigenous majority were scathing in their denunciations of the culprits, 'It wasn't reight,' they agreed. 'Nobody had any business to do that' – not to our mosque.

6
Paradise Lost

MILTON (as someone said), thou shouldst be living at this hour. Because it would take at least a Milton's pen to do justice to the exclusion from Paradise which was signalled by my first day at Field Lane Infants' School. No great iron doors clanged shut with eternal reverberations as I entered its portals. No angel threatened me with a flaming sword on the day when, all unsuspecting and acccompanied by my ever-solicitous mother, I went to meet the headmistress.

On the contrary, I was beguiled with false promises of bliss. While my mother chatted with a small, black-clad woman called Miss Terry, I pushed wheeled toys about the floor under the delightful illusion that from now on they would be mine, all mine, to play with. Miss Terry's professional smiles inspired in me no reason to doubt that a new and exciting era was opening before me.

The reality proved somewhat different. No longer could I wander all day in and out of the houses in Albert Street, conversing precociously with indulgent, warm-hearted neighbours, and blissfully safe, while my sister was at school, from forced participation in games with her sloppy friends. Now I too was at school, even if it was only 'The Babies', as the youngest class at Field Lane was misleadingly called. It included some unappealing kids with unpredictable tempers.

If I played in the sandpit, they wanted to play in the sandpit – with, of course, whatever I happened to have in my hand. Since assertiveness has never been my strong point I usually let them have what they wanted and thus was soon recognised as 'soft' (long a West Riding synonym for tolerant).

I was also incurably dreamy and prone to mind-wandering, which perhaps explains why I found it difficult to concentrate on tasks like learning how to lace up shoes with the aid of a mock-up of a shoe's 'upper'. And I was slow – at least in movement. All this recollection of my early failings makes me wonder how I survived at all, especially since my dreaminess frequently took a wishful turn. Then, under the impression that school had surely gone on long enough for one day, I would set off for home at playtime, only to be called back by my more alert schoolmates, who had spotted me through the playground railing, purposefully homeward bound.

Despite all this, I found myself prematurely promoted from The Babies to the 'First Class' (an apparent anomaly that was not wasted on me even at that early age). Miss Terry or Miss Coultas or one of the other flower-smocked attendant angels must have seen beyond my difficulty with lace-holes and a propensity to mistake playtime for home-time. Could they have decided that here were talents to nurture? Or was it simply that they couldn't decide what the dickens to do with me next since they could see no future for me at all?

They never consulted me, or I could have offered them a variety of choices. Regrettably I was too young to join the Army or the Navy, even though I was already kitted out with my father's old service cap from 'The Tigers' (the York and Lancaster Regiment) plus a German soldier's water bottle he had picked up on some foreign field. Even at my most optimistic I would not have considered myself a candidate for sporting fame. But I did rather fancy myself as an explorer, due, no doubt, to the presence on our wall at Albert Street of two ancient framed lithographs of Stanley and Livingstone.

Stanley, I remember, wore a military-looking solar topee and a dauntless expression, and despite the fact that the sober-looking Dr Livingstone was a missionary and therefore a proper subject for respect, if not veneration, it was Sir Henry M. Stanley who won my admiration. But all this speculation is purely academic, since in those days the aspirations of small boys were rarely taken seriously – especially small boys who often seemed uncertain what day it was.

To be fair to myself, whilst I sometimes lost track of the days in the middle of the week, I was never in doubt about the two that came at the end, perhaps because in character they were at least as different from each other as Stanley and Livingstone. After the morning chores of shopping for my mother at the Co-op in Taylor Street, where I was served by the jovial Albert (never at a loss for a spot of banter with small boys or lady customers), Saturday came into its own as the Stanley of the pair, adventurous and freedom-loving. On Saturday I could wander in the woods and fields, invariably incurring my mother's wrath when I returned home with half the countryside on my shoes and clothes. Yes, Saturday was Stanley's day all right: Sunday, to my taste, had far too much in common with Livingstone. Make too much noise on that day and you were asked in tones of outrage, 'Don't y'know it's Sunday?' and told how, on Sundays in your parents' childhood, everything, with the possible exception of breathing very quietly, was forbidden.

Sunday began with morning service, which included an address for children, after which came a sermon, admittedly short (though quite long enough in my view) for the adults. Then it was home for Sunday dinner, probably Yorkshire pudding first (on its own, of course, supposedly on the theory that this reduced your appetite for the meat and vegetables which followed. Or is that merely a southern slander?). During the meal I wore a white apron, an optimistic device of my mother's to protect my Sunday suit.

Before you knew it, it was time for Sunday school, where after more hymns we were required to read the Bible in turn and had our short-trousered legs slapped for any unruly behaviour. Home for tea, then in no time at all you were setting off for evening service, which often ended with the hymn 'The day Thou gavest, Lord, is ended', always, to my ears a melancholy lament for the poor weekend which seemed to have died so tragically young.

The only thing that relieved the tedium of Sunday was the company of my cousin Leonard. A few months my senior, Leonard was out-going, talkative and innocently ingratiating; an only child who was everything I was not and yet my closest boyhood friend. We cheerfully competed for the same girls' affections, discussed the deepest (and the most nonsensical) questions and could truthfully be said to have had no secrets from each other.

Having two sons so near in age, our mothers, while almost as close as sisters on the surface, eyed each other's progeny with a protective, though usually suppressed, jealousy. When Leonard won a scholarship to the local Technical College, his mother (my Aunt Clara) proudly told mine that the Principle had confided to her that his school got 'the cream' of the local boys, a piece of news which my mother received without noticeable elation.

Leonard, though to all appearances overflowing with health, was always in and out of hospital, including the local isolation hospital; though what took him there I cannot remember. I do know that for all his unfailing cheerfulness the mere antiseptic 'hospital' smell was enough to induce in him a near-nauseous terror.

With his luck, it was almost inevitable that when his mother bought him a bicycle (much tutting by relatives, who said, 'She spoils that lad'), he should have an accident, brought on by skylarking with another young cyclist, and break his arm. The operation, for some reason, left him disabled, with one arm permanently fixed in a right-angle at the elbow.

I pitied Leonard for having grumpy Uncle Isaac as his father. When I was small and insisting on outstaying my welcome at Leonard's house near the chapel after morning service, Uncle Isaac would take the unpardonable liberty of smacking my legs. He never made rabbit hutches or kites for Leonard, as my father did for me. But perhaps Uncle Isaac, who had not worked for years and spent much of his time sitting in front of the

My father 'on the trams' during the thirties.

Skylarking with his pals somewhere 'over there' during World War I. Dad is on the extreme right.

Mother in happy mood on a chapel outing to a pleasure garden.

Top left: My youngest uncle, Willie, who joined up, characteristically under-age.
Right: Every inch a soldier – Uncle Frederick.
Bottom left: My maternal grandmother.

Left: My uncles Walter and Ernest in World War I. Top right: When cricket was cricket – on the beach at Scarborough. Below: We joined the Navy.

Top left: Dad's photograph of Knaresborough.
Right: Dad and me in the yard below 'our eccentric little house' in Albert Street.
Below: Mother's orange box garden on the steps to our door, complete with Dad's gate to prevent me straying.

Overleaf: Mother and Dad in later years.

Singing in opera. Brenda, aged seventeen, when she played Antonia in a local production of Tales of Hoffman.

At Scarborough in the late fifties with Brenda, daughter Anne and son Peter.

fire smoking tobacco economically mixed with dried tea-leaves, had reason
to be grumpy. He had never been a soldier, like my dad, no doubt because
he had a club foot. And while Leonard was still hardly more than a
youth, Uncle Isaac was found to have cancer: he died after a long and
painful illness.

My mother was present when Leonard visited him just before, or just
after, the end. 'Leonard did something you wouldn't have done,' she told
me, with sudden, unexpected reproach. 'He kissed his father.' I could find
no answer. It has never been easy for me to demonstrate affection and
strangely that knowledge somehow took the sting from her words, though
not the surprise that for once she had compared the two of us to my
disadvantage. Leonard's damaged arm kept him out of the Services and
therefore may conceivably have saved his life though he was not destined
for a long one. He fell victim to the cardiac weakness which afflicted my
father's side of the family and died in his middle thirties.

The good, they say, die young, inducing sober reflections, perhaps, in
those of us who tend to hang around rather longer.

ALTHOUGH my mother seemed strangely proud of my premature promotion in my early days at Field Lane School, it meant all too little to me.
My new status seemed to offer no advantages whatever. Even the doubtful
pleasures of the sandpit were now out of reach and other activities which
might have been expected to add pleasure to life invariably proved to have
a worm in the bud.

Take the percussion band, whose repertoire, as I recall it, seemed to
run to one tune only, *In an English Country Garden*. In this jolly ditty we
accompanied Miss Coultas's piano on drums, triangles and various other
noise-producing instruments with much banging and tinkling. Yet while
I knew I could have produced the bangs on the drum with a joyful gusto,
all they allotted me was a few pings of the triangle. Such experiences
leave their mark on a man – even at the age of six and a half. Triangles,
as everyone knew, were for girls. They were certainly not *me*, whereas
the drum decidedly was. Or so I thought. How could I make them see
that my natural spontaneous love for that instrument must inevitably be
accompanied by an equivalent talent?

But if what passed for music was not seen as my forte, at least I was
always the best 'reader' in the class, the best at grammar, too, as far as
it was taught. Had it not been for my execrable handwriting I might have
been reckoned the best in 'composition', as indeed I was in later years.
Unfortunately, where I really excelled was in making a fool of myself – not
without a little help, I might add, from some of the less sensitive members
of staff.

I was afflicted, for instance, with what is now called 'mirror-writing',

writing certain letters and figures the 'wrong' way round. Perhaps the root of the problem lay in my inability to see that it mattered which way you wrote a figure 2 or a letter B. But apparently it did, and while my failings in the matter were seen as serious faults, there was clearly much humorous mileage to be gained when the teacher felt inclined to it. Thus I would be summoned to the front of the class, handed the chalk and instructed to write the appropriate letter or figure. In such a situation I inevitably got it wrong.

My single happy memory of Field Lane School is of my first Christmas there. 'Magic' is too hackneyed a term to describe what that enchanted season already meant and to some extent will always mean to me. At home, the pillow cases left for Santa Claus to fill (stockings were too small even in our straitened household). The offerings, left for this, the only significant saint in our Protestant calendar – were spice cake and ginger wine (the non-alcoholic kind, need I add?).

Our little artificial Christmas tree with its perennial ornaments was unearthed year after year, and every year better loved. It bloomed and flourished as we all did in the scent of Dad's cigar, an annual luxury bought by my sister and me with sacrificially saved pennies – not always willingly saved on my part, though I knew that any self-indulgence on sweets or toy soldiers in the weeks leading up to Christmas would let me in for a tedious lecture from big sister Vera on my filial obligations.

And of course, there was the carol singing . . .

'GO away an' play till Christmas,' called a voice through the door, still unopened despite a second knock from the juvenile carollers. My sister and her friends collapsed in giggles – girls would laugh at owt! But there were weeks to go yet before Christmas, and the girls thought the remark the funniest thing they'd heard since the last Laurel and Hardy film at the Regent pictures.

My introduction to this now sadly withered custom of carolling was of course engineered by my sister, who was as sociable, enterprising and energetic as I was lacking in such qualities. A reluctant recruit, yet again, to the invariably female posse, I would be taken on a round of neighbours' houses to help perform the familiar repertoire of so-called carols before signing off with 'We wish you a merry Christmas and a happy new year, *A* new year, *A* new year,' and so on.

We were merciless in giving good value, never halting until we'd sung the last syllable and note we knew. Nowadays, if kids go carolling at all, you're lucky (or unlucky) maybe, to get more than a couple of tuneless stanzas before a hectoring knock heralds a demand for alms. But at least we had not yet been infected by the obnoxious American virus of 'Trick or Treat'! That bare-faced exercise in demanding money with menaces was doubtless a feature of the childhood of Al Capone. Perhaps he started it.

We, on the other hand, offered no more than a musical threat – and that with the most innocent intentions. Usually the door would be opened in response to our knock and a few coppers more or less graciously bestowed and thankfully received. Doubtless to my selfish disgust, our share of the corporate booty went straight into my sister's Christmas fund for parents.

Back at Field Lane School, the Christmas trimmings we'd been creating for weeks from tortured coloured paper wreathed the windows and festooned the lights. The emphasis on work (even in the First Class) seemed to have eased and we'd been singing *I saw three ships come sailing in, on Christmas Day in the morning*, while Miss Coultas played the piano.

I liked the tune. It was strangely refreshing after 'Good King Wenceslas' (irreverently satirised as 'Good King Wenc'las knocked a bobby senseless right in the middle of Marks and Spencers'). But my logical West Riding mind jibbed at what followed: 'And who was in those ships all three? Our Saviour Christ and his Laydee on Christmas Day in the morning.' Since Christ was born in a stable on Christmas Day how could he have been sailing in any ship – let alone three – on the same day?

What happened next gave me no intellectual problems, only a sense of incredulous wonder at the most amazing pre-Christmas marvel of all – the three sticky boiled sweets neatly placed on a tiny square of drawing paper on the desk before each child. Miss Coultas, wonder of wonders, had sent out some trusty to Mr Hartley's shop across the road and had actually paid for the treat with her own money!

Could this be the same Miss Coultas who had amazingly smacked my legs for talking when we were all lined up after playtime, ready to march into school for more dreary lessons? After similarly chastising another offender, she had added the final crushing, unanswerable rebuke, 'And your father a *policeman*!' Yes, it was the same Miss Coultas and none other. Verily, Christmas was Christmas, even at school.

ONCE again it's Christmas Eve and I am lying in bed at Albert Street. No central heating then, but if the night is especially frosty, perhaps a paraffin stove. It gives off a strangely exciting, comforting smell and through the fretted top of its metal case the flame from its circular wick throws fantastic patterns on the ceiling. It had to be really cold before we could have 'the stove on' – paraffin wasn't cheap. But at Christmas an exception might be made.

Often during the long twilit evenings of summer my fancy had peopled the darkening purple gloom with ghosts which were usually dispelled by 'havin' t'wireless on'. For Dad had wired up the old horn loudspeaker in my bedroom when he bought a new and bigger one for use downstairs. This technological triumph usually sent me happily to sleep or awakened my protests if he switched the extension off while I was still awake. Variety shows were my favourites, with comedians who had me rolling helplessly about my bed. It was different when what Dad called 'chamber music', with its wailing strings and wordless, often mournful themes seemed to reawaken the terrors of *The Double Door* or *The Mummy's Curse*, unwisely absorbed at the Regent Cinema the night before.

But though Christmas was traditionally the season for ghosts, that was when I dreaded them least; for then they were ruthlessly exorcised by much happier spirits whose voices carried far on the frosty air. At first I heard them faintly, the male and female singers of the chapel choirs in rich, unaccompanied harmony.

Christians, awake came first. Then, perhaps, *While shepherds watched*, sung, according to West Riding tradition and with no sense of incongruity, to the tune more often sung to the words of *Ilkla' Moor baht 'at*. Could it have happened anywhere but in Yorkshire? But as the wiseacres would assure you, the so-called Yorkshire anthem was originally improvised on some nineteenth-century choir outing to a popular hymn-tune of the time whose first purpose has now been practically forgotten – except in Yorkshire.

Christmas Eve in childhood must be as close as most of us get to heaven, certainly in this life. Never again shall I lie so still or peaceably in bed as I did then. Those nights, in retrospect at least, were invariably moonlit and dusted with enough frost (or snow, if youthful prayers were answered) to bring a tingle to the cheeks of the singers and make a small boy, listening in bed, even warmer.

The sound of the singing would swell or fade as the touring choirs moved nearer or farther away. Finally, one choir was discerned to be drawing ever closer: *our* choir was coming to sing at our house . . .

The clatter of feet along the stone setts in the street outside finally ceased. There followed a moment of silence, then John Gillings, the choirmaster, would raise his hand and they would start to sing. And Christmas began.

7

I just miss
t' dip'theria

UNCLE Jack and Auntie Grace were staying with us when I was in
bed with tonsilitis. Uncle Jack was my mother's brother and Grace
was his second wife. They lived in Rotherham, near Sheffield,
whither Jack had gone in search of better prospects, after spending his early
life helping Grandad Poole to sell paraffin from a horse and cart. They had
a daughter called Dora who was quite a prodigy as a pianist. I think she
finally became a teacher.

I liked Uncle Jack, even though he insisted on giving me whiskery kisses
when I met him at the bus stop. My mother idolised him all her life as her
wonderful, jolly elder brother Jack until he died in his eighties. But I
always felt that Grace, a brisk, good-natured, go-ahead sort of woman,
possibly made my mother feel slow or old-fashioned.

Compared with Rotherham, a sort of mini-Sheffield, Batley was something of a backwater. Jack and Grace and Dora lived in a suburb in a house
which seemed ultra-modern and smart when compared with our eccentric
little home in Batley. At Rotherham their indoor W.C. alone was enough
to impress us, though when we stayed with them I was for some reason
repeatedly warned not to 'flush it'.

What good was a posh indoor lavatory, I wondered, if you couldn't flush
it? Ours may have been the best part of fifty yards away from the house,
but it usually worked – except, of course, in winter when it was often
'frozzen up'. Then we had to turn the water off and send for the plumber,
hoping that he wouldn't be long in coming – though with so many other
outdoor lavatories all 'frozzen up' at once, it might be days before he got
round to ours.

Uncle Jack came to see us once or twice a year and sometimes we went
to Rotherham. While we were there we would visit Grace's parents,
Grandpa Emery, a tall commanding ex-policeman, and Grandma Emery,

along with a few other friends and relations of the Rotherham set. In some hardly definable way they seemed as engagingly different from what we knew at home as their indoor lavatories and electric light.

Grandpa Emery was an almost Dickensian character, prone to sententious utterances. One day he found my sister reading a copy of *Peg's Paper* she had picked up somewhere. Towering above her, he pronounced: 'A woman is known by the literature she reads'. Then, his verdict delivered, he strode away evidently satisfied with his performance.

Whatever Grandpa Emery thought about us, Uncle Jack and his family were clearly happy to have us visit them – that was their nature – but I thought it a pity that Uncle Jack had to work so much at home in the evenings, sitting at a little desk full of papers. He was an insurance agent, whatever that meant, and, in addition, I think, ran clubs through which people bought all kinds of things on instalments.

I knew the Rotherham relations had more money than we had, or how could they give me two new half crown pieces, five whole shillings, for Christmas? At first I thought the coins must be made of chocolate covered with silver paper, and almost took a fork to them to investigate. But it never entered my head to begrudge the Rotherham folk their more affluent state. Anyway, being well off hardly seemed worth while if you had to work in the evenings.

How we fitted the three of them into our little house when I had tonsilitis I have never worked out. Mother and Dad slept downstairs, having presumably brought their bed down into the living room, and I slept there too, on a settee which could be opened out to make a bed. Somehow or other, Uncle Jack, Auntie Grace, Dora and my sister Vera were accommodated upstairs.

Not only had I tonsilitis, but rheumatism, too, a fact the kids at school found extremely amusing as everybody knew it was something only old folk got. But I had it all right and it was so painful that for a time I could not bear even the weight of a sheet on my arms.

Diphtheria then was much more of a scourge than it is today. Our doctor, a quiet young Scot, was afraid I might be starting with that, too, so he took swabs from my throat and sent them away somewhere to be analysed. It was either before or after this that he gave me The Injection, which, I was assured, was to make me better. I should have known what to expect when the bedclothes were pulled back and on the doctor's instructions, my parents, Uncle Jack and Auntie Grace each took hold of an arm or a leg. Then the kind and gentle doctor inserted a needle into my side.

From that first gasping moment when the point punctured my flesh, seeming to enter my deepest vitals I was in a world apart – separate from that of the doctor who was causing the pain, from my vicariously suffering parents, and from little Dora standing solemn-faced with her parents and mine around the bed. Probably the operation lasted moments only but it felt unending as the needle seemed to search around in my side for ever more painful points to penetrate.

I didn't sleep much that night: my side was too sore. But next day I found myself something of a hero. Neighbours popped in to commiserate and offer suggestions for my improvement. One of them brought a huge orange. Auntie Grace, not to be outdone, thought a nice juicy peach – or 'perch', as little Dora called it to everyone's vast amusement – might tempt my languishing appetite.

The neighbours didn't exactly light bonfires or dance with glee, but it was perfectly clear that everyone in Albert Street knew and rejoiced that Jinny's little lad had 'just missed dip'theria'.

8

Crime and punishment

I F I had hated Field Lane Infants' School, I found Warwick Road Elementary School even more of a trial. I certainly went there with no sense of promotion in life. The 'big school', I guessed, would be much like the junior school, only worse. I found no reason to change my view.

The school was on the edge of what was then a slum area and many of its pupils were as rough as you might have expected. Generally speaking, the teachers saw it as their duty to tame as much as to teach their pupils. The father of one lad, good-natured to all appearances but incurably trouble-prone, once told the Headmaster, 'I can't do owt with 'im, so yer mun do t' best yer can. I shan't complain whatever you do'. Given such licence, the Head saw it as his duty to act as vigorously as necessary *in loco parentis*.

Most male teachers used canes, with the exception of one, who would clout a lad about the head with the flat of his hand for minor mis-demeanours, only resorting to the stick (which he would borrow from another teacher) to punish what he considered serious crime. Later some teachers forsook canes for straps, a development that exercised my mind a good deal. I was sure they hadn't done it from any humanitarian motive. Perhaps, I reasoned, some boy had suffered some injury, such as a broken finger, when being caned and the teachers were scared of the retribution such an incident might bring upon them.

Whether sticks, canes or even the flat of the hand were really necessary to maintain discipline I cannot say. Few were prepared to risk dispensing with them. Certainly, with the exception of one brief and heavily punished attempt, teachers were virtually safe from attack at my school. Not even the biggest of boys dared, except on that one occasion, to raise a hand against the smallest of teachers. Yet it was not unknown for an irate father to appear at school after one of his children had been punished or in some way res-tricted. When a father serving in the local Territorials arrived, demanding that his son leave lessons early in order to accompany the battalion to their annual camp, the Head acted in his customary ex-officer manner.

'Lock the door, Mr Bishop, and send for the police,' he told the caretaker. To the father he added, 'I'm all in favour of boys going with their fathers to camp but there'll be plenty of time after school is finished.' To my great disappointment the father capitulated, and what promised to have been an exciting episode proved something of a damp squib.

On one or two occasions during my stay at Warwick Road the partitions would be drawn back and the whole school (or probably, and significantly, just the boys) would stand in the manner of Captain Bligh's crew witnessing a quarterdeck flogging. I cannot even remember what the crimes were which merited such public severity. Neither, although any diversion was welcome, can I recall that this solemn event produced any great excitement. No doubt the Head first told us why he was doing it and thought his action was for the ultimate good of all.

After that the offender would be placed over a desk and the cane or strap applied vigorously to the seat of his pants while the rest of us watched, wavering between admiration and sympathy for the culprit. I don't remember being stirred to any great resolve to avoid anything that might end with me lying bottom-up over a desk with my fellow pupils witnessing my humiliation. Anyway, I knew I was unlikely to be involved in the sort of scrapes that led to such treatment.

Much later in my life a great friend of mine, then in his fifties, recalled a public flogging he had undergone at a grammar school in another town after being falsely accused of theft. For years after, he could never bring himself to speak of the event and I suspect that when he described it to me it may have been the first time in forty years that he had revealed to anyone the utter confusion and baseless guilt it had left in his mind.

I would have accepted without hesitation in those days the proposition that all teachers were sadists, even if I had yet to encounter the word. Why else should they cane me for getting my sums wrong? I'd been getting them wrong all my life, or at least since I encountered long division. I could usually work out the problem 'in my head' – it was the 'working' on paper that never 'worked' for me. But how could they believe that inflicting physical pain would clarify the problem? They must cane me because it gave them pleasure.

Well, now and then, perhaps, they off-loaded anger and frustration on us. But more often, I am sure, we were simply victims of the official view that if you couldn't do the work, you weren't 'trying' and must therefore suffer – for your own ultimate good. But surely they should have seen that it didn't work – at least with me.

Was all this reflected in the pupils' attitude to violence? Certainly fights were everyday occurrences and usually took place after school on the secluded venue of Henry Street, conveniently close to the school but hidden by buildings from passing teachers' eyes. I never 'appeared' as a contestant in any of these major encounters, which might be attended by half the boys in the school – and a good few of the girls, too, I dare say. My own fights were mere brief skirmishes, from which I extricated myself as quickly and painlessly as possible.

The trouble was that somehow I couldn't avoid getting into them, partly because I couldn't keep my mouth shut, though I was unable or unwilling to back it up with my fists. Furthermore, I knew that getting involved in a fight after school would certainly delay my arrival home and I was much more afraid of facing my infuriated mother than of settling with any other antagonist.

It wasn't always easy to extricate myself. On the way to battle the popular contestant (rarely, if ever, me) would be escorted by his supporters in the manner of a world title contender with his entourage. For a few brief moments he was a hero and unwilling to relinquish his glory before he had to. On the contrary, he hoped to increase and extend it by knocking eight bells out of me.

Looking back on my life I can now see that I could have saved myself untold trouble merely by wearing a smile and avoiding disputation. But to wear a smile at school when you hated the very smell of the place was less than easy, and to fall in with what, rightly or wrongly, I considered inferior manners, speech and customs seemed cowardly and weak, a yielding to temptation which was just as reprehensible as falling for the blandishments of the demon drink, as colourfully represented to us at the weekly Band of Hope meeting. In short, I suppose I was a a terrible little snob, though I'd have indignantly denied the charge: snobs were people with lots of brass who talked posh.

It was simply that the Colbecks knew best, and no-one knew better than our parents. That being the case, until I reached my teens it rarely occurred to me to rebel. It just wasn't worth it. Had I not been convinced of this I might have been spared the episode of the umbrella.

Today, I find it almost incredible that a) I was prevailed upon to accept such an intolerable situation and b) that my unquestionably loving mother could have failed to see just how unbearable it was.

It happened on one of those days in the summers of my childhood when, after weeks of sweltering sunshine, the skies would blacken, the thunder roll and finally the clouds would let fall on the parched pavements and withering grass a bouncing, streaming, drenching downpour, whose novelty delighted us kids, though not my mother.

She was certain that, having no raincoat that I had not outgrown, I would get 'wet through' with dire consequences on my mile-long walk to school. Suddenly, and with a smile of triumph, she produced – an umbrella! I looked at it in the certainty that I was having a nightmare.

It had belonged to one of my grandfathers, already deceased. It was black and vaguely threatening, with a hooked handle. As protection for an Independent Methodist attending a funeral of one of the faithful it would have been just the thing, but as a ten-year-old boy on his way to school, I felt it just 'wasn't me'. Nor could it possibly be anybody else under ninety! The other kids would laugh, I protested weakly, well knowing that this sort of argument never carried an ounce of weight. If they laughed, my mother said, they were 'silly'. And anyway, the opinions of children, all of whom were silly by definition, didn't matter at all to my mother, no matter how much they did to me!

My sister was laughing already as we set out on the long road to school. Within minutes we were separated as a crowd of delighted children, hooting with mirth, surrounded me. I had never known there were so many kids at our school and clearly not one of them had ever seen anything so indescribably comic as me with my umbrella. It left the circus procession, even with elephants and clowns, completely out of sight.

Useless for me even to attempt to point out the advantages bestowed by this incredible instrument. Warnings like 'It'll be you that gets pneumonia, not me' left the mockers as unmoved as I had known they would. Occasional offensive sallies, using the brolly as a weapon, were equally ineffectual. The danger of having it snatched from my grasp, never to be seen again, was all too real. It was bad enough having to take the thing to school – to arrive home without it would not have helped.

What I did with it when we got to school I have no idea. I only remember that there the teachers, too, joined in the jollity. The obvious place to leave my brolly was, of course, the cloakroom, where the hook it hung on surely deserves a commemorative plaque inscribed 'Here hung the only umbrella ever to be carried by a pupil to this school'.

The homeward journey proved much less traumatic. By that time the kids had developed something of an affection for my umbrella, perhaps because it had enlivened their schoolward journey as nothing ever had before. They may even have felt a wondering respect for a fellow pupil who could do anything so utterly unbelievable. On my homeward way the torrents were renewed. Now the kids clustered under my brolly and, like a missionary surrounded by converts, I led them splashing through the puddles to the strains of 'Tipperary' and 'Pack up your troubles in your old kitbag'.

As I progressed, if that's the word, through the 'big school' it was gradually recognised that the only thing I was any good at was 'English', and though this was seen as a pretty doubtful sort of accomplishment it might as well be encouraged. Hence Hermon Hall's well-meant advice that I 'ought to be a writer when I grew up'; and the dispensation by another teacher, Cicero Armitage, to me and a class-mate (who in due course himself became a journalist) that we might choose our own 'composition' subjects.

Due to a slight degree of overcrowding in the class at that time, a table had been brought into the room and placed at one corner. Here the future editor of the *Brighouse Echo*, Kenneth Cassidy, and I would sit in solitary splendour during the afternoons devoted to English and write by permission about whatever came into our heads. Like a couple of juvenile aesthetes we compared notes and discussed each other's creations and doubtless became rather conceited.

As the years passed, another umbrella became even more famous than mine had, though nowhere near as much fun. It belonged to a man called Neville Chamberlain, who seemed to spend much of his time trotting about Europe to meet Mussolini or Hitler. The world was heading for war, but the fact did not yet greatly affect our lives. On one afternoon a week we trekked to 'the field', an area of tussocky grassland alongside a railway line. Here, those of us disinclined to ball games or superfluous to team requirements would play a game of our own invention, originally called 'Italians and Abbysinians', during which we would skirmish and pelt each other with small stones.

Came the day when the civilian population was issued with gas masks – 'respirators', as the headmaster insisted on calling them – and the war began to loom larger on our youthful horizons. But the event which made most impact on me was the decision, made with air raids in mind, that any child living more than a certain distance from school – it may have been a mile or two miles – should stay at home.

What joy! There was obviously something to be said for war after all. Whether or not I lived outside the stipulated limit, I certainly insisted that I did, and since my fourteenth birthday fell in the very month, September 1939, that Neville Chamberlain gravely told the country we were 'at war with Germany', I had my way. It still puzzles me that all the scallywags and dunces who might have been expected to rejoice even more than I at this heaven-sent dispensation, insisted on going to school no matter how far away they lived.

9
Nature boy

MY first contact with animals was hardly encouraging. 'Shake 'ands wi' t' little lad,' Mrs Hepworth, who lived on the top yard, had instructed her brown collie dog.

Aged no more than four, I was being taken on a tour of neighbours' houses and the introduction was made in all good faith, my mother's pride in her small son being almost equalled by Mrs Hepworth's pride in her dog. On the face of it, there seemed no reason why we two should not be the best of friends.

But the dog saw no reason why we should.

'Come on! Shake 'ands,' insisted Mrs Hepworth. Utterly trustful I offered my own small paw, whereupon the dog leapt forward and took a neat bite out of my forehead, leaving a scar above the left eyebrow that remains to this day. I howled, my mother gasped with horror and Mrs Hepworth laid into the poor, jealous collie, which retreated in disgrace into the house.

I can imagine my mother's face as she cut short Mr and Mrs Hepworths' apologies and hurried me, still howling, down the street and up the steps to our house. At the door, she remembered with horror that Dad was not at home – he had taken my sister to a cricket match of all things! Just like a man . . . Fortunately, he soon returned home to administer first aid to me (which was easy) and reassurance to my mother (rather more difficult).

Despite all the consternation, which no doubt made the episode far more traumatic than it need have been, the experience left me with no fear of animals. On the contrary, I have been fascinated by them all my life. Dogs and cats recognise me on sight as a soft touch, always good for a pat and a stroke or a handout. Why this should be I'm at a loss to know. I ruthlessly incarcerated newts and fish and birds with an enthusiasm that far outweighed any consideration for the animals' wishes in the matter. Like most kids I was a show-off, encouraging a naive tendency on the part of neighbours and relations to turn me into a miniature celebrity. My mother, glad to find any quality of mine that she could boast about, joined in. Going for a walk with me, she would say, with a pride that ought really to have made me blush, was as good as going 'Out with Romany'.

'Romany', the Reverend G. Bramwell Evans, was famous in my childhood as a broadcaster on Children's Hour on the BBC's North Region and as a writer and lecturer. An ordained Methodist minister, related, I was told, to a famous evangelist of the time called Gipsy Smith, Romany was certainly not a Romany in name alone. His brown face, thick eyebrows, flashing teeth and black hair convinced you of that.

When he lectured in local chapels he would make lightning charcoal sketches of the creatures he was describing. Sometimes, unknown to the audience, his dog, Raq, a Cocker Spaniel which obviously worshipped him, came along too. At the end of the lecture, a door would be opened and the dog, which had been kept waiting in the porch, would hurtle like a bullet the length of the building, bound up the steps to the pulpit and fling itself into Romany's arms, an event which brought the house down – or as nearly as possible in such decorous surroundings.

Romany was as much a humorist as he was a naturalist. On the air, with no more than a microphone and a couple of Children's Hour 'Aunties' as companions, he could entertainingly transport his listeners from places like Albert Street, of which there was no shortage in the North, to the seashore and the cliffs above Whitby. There, for at least part of the time, he lived in his *vardo* (the Romany word, as he explained to his listeners, for what we *Gorgios* call a caravan). His popularity demonstrated how keenly in the most industrial areas human beings hungered for the peace and beauty of the countryside.

Many years were to pass before I sat in a Budapest nightclub as one of a party of visiting journalists that included – who else but the daughter of the BBC's Romany, herself bearing the Christian name Romany and wearing impressive earrings that matched her name. Somehow or other the Gipsy orchestra, one of the most famous in Hungary, we were told, learned that one of their own was in our group. She spoke a few words to them in the Romany tongue and showed them a photograph of her grandparents standing proudly in traditional dress at the door of their vardo. From that moment, our table was 'in'.

The party went on till 4 a.m. while the Tzigane musicians played every English tune they knew. Liszt and Strauss alternated with 'Daisy' and 'Pack up your troubles'. An inveterate Romany fan, my mother would have loved it, though I doubt if she would have been tempted to sample the Tokay we were drinking, or approved the hour at which we returned to our hotel.

Had she known it, during Romany's heyday in the thirties, there was really a big difference between going 'Out with Romany' and going out with me – Romany knew what he was talking about, whereas I was inclined to overlay the facts of our discoveries with a varnish of fancy, based on the half-digested books I borrowed from our public library. If I didn't know for certain what we had discovered I would make a hopeful guess at the most exciting alternative I could think of.

Ever since my sister used to smuggle me into the junior library behind her while I was still under the magic age of eight and had to cower out of sight below the librarian's counter, I have been an inveterate book borrower. Occasionally I would spoil her plan by standing up too soon and being ejected.

They never had to eject my Uncle Isaac. A rather grumpy Christian socialist of the old school, he declined to enter the place for years. Having been endowed by the millionaire Andrew Carnegie, it was nothing better, he would tell you, than the product of sweated labour. But I was quite uninfluenced by this somewhat embittered man, who scandalised the congregation in hot weather by sitting in chapel minus collar or tie. God, as Uncle Isaac knew perfectly well, had no time for such fripperies and had the Almighty suddenly appeared there was every likelihood that, if the day were hot, He, too, would be just as casually attired.

Lacking Uncle Isaac's scruples about sweated labour, I continued to visit the library to borrow works by Victorian clergymen who had apparently little to do but imprison fishes and reptiles in glass tanks, or fill cabinets with butterflies or birds' eggs. These they would write about in learned phrases, larded with Latin, that I would repeat and usually mispronounce. It was, though I didn't know it at the time, as much an education for me to unravel their academic sentences as my absorption via the hymnbook of the English of Watts and Wesley, or my exposure to Haydn and Handel while pumping the organ for the chapel oratorios. My conscious mind may have been more concerned with the latest young female recruit to the choir, but on the whole the musical love affairs lasted longer.

I was uneasily aware that my own performance as a naturalist was rather on the academic side compared with that of some of my schoolmates – always, it seemed, the 'rougher' element, who went birdsnesting and could show you eggs in plenty to prove their prowess. When I went with them, feeling not quite at home, the bushes they searched never failed to hold a nest, whose treasures they rifled with none of the restraint preached by the books that I read and they ignored. 'Never take more than one egg' was a rule I hardly dared to preach, but had always followed. Alas, on one occasion . . .

'Ther's one in 'ere,' shouted Tishy Senior, typically in the lead. Sure enough, a hedge sparrow, having sat tight until the last second, flew protesting from the nest, revealing a clutch of blue eggs which grubby, thorn-scratched hands soon reduced to one only. Typically bringing up the rear,

I was faced with probably the biggest temptation of my short life – the biggest and the briefest. Today I feel even guiltier than I did then about taking that one remaining egg.

At the age of eleven or thereabouts my seriously declared ambition was to write a book 'about frogs', which peculiarly enchanted me. Hardly surprising that I got a premature reputation as 'a funny lad'. To be over-fond of what most people saw as creepy-crawlies or 'vermin', in the West Riding of my youth was hardly a highway to popularity. As my father-in-law was prone to demand many years later, while unwillingly watching wild life programmes on television, "What good are they?' His sentence on anything that was not obviously of service to mankind was 'Gas 'em!', while to allow anything to live (much less be preserved) that could endanger human life was to him nothing short of idiotic.

More recently I have flattered myself that I was in good, or at least distinguished company, for Yorkshire eccentrics (who must, of course, by definition, be the best of their kind) have often had a weakness for animals – and animals for them. Take Jemmy Hirst or Squire Waterton, two of the greatest in Yorkshire's gallery of famous oddities. Jemmy used to ride a bull to hounds. He taught a rooster to dance to his mouth organ and a duck to swim backwards. He was a much coarser-grained character than Waterton, though no one would have denied both of them the title of eccentric (except, perhaps, the squire himself, who always insisted, in the teeth of the evidence, that he was the most commonplace of men).

One of Waterton's best-loved pets was a duck born with its head reversed, which had to turn a somersault in order to seize food he placed for it on the ground. Both he and Jemmy Hirst, without noticeable success, attempted to fly with home-made wings. I can hardly claim an exploit quite so daring, though like Jemmy I more than once encouraged dogs to follow me to school so that I might be ordered to remove them, a task I hardly hurried over.

Trespassing in spring in the local rookery, I found the ground littered with fledgeling rooks which had fallen from the nest and perished, since their parents were not equipped by nature either to notice their disappearance or to do anything about it.

Then, with excitement, I noticed that one of these small black creatures was alive. I could feel my heart beating as I bent to pick it up, though my excitement had possibly less to do with life-saving zeal than with the prospect of enlarging my reputation and my menagerie at a stroke. It gaped at me, whether in self-defence or a demand for food I didn't know – or care. I only knew that somehow or other I must get this blue-black, bright-eyed creature back to Albert Street.

Seeing me carrying it proudly up the street, my mother, who was perilously washing the windows while seated on the sill, her legs pinned down inside by the sash, lamented that she had enough mouths to feed already.

'It'll not eat much,' I coaxed her, and of course it didn't. Once its presence was known to the rest of the street, the offerings brought by neighbours' children – everything from centipedes to wine gums – would have been enough to choke, let alone sustain it.

Co-operative as ever, Dad adapted the shed he had built for my rabbits and guinea pigs as a cage, installing a length of broom handle as a perch. Soon, however, Jim, as I called him with a certain lack of originality, was leading a life of almost complete freedom as one of the family. Having learned to fly, he would soar as high as the roof tops or follow me on foot up and down the street, cawing in protest and flying a few yards if I walked too fast. In the morning, when his cage door was opened, he would hop purposefully up the eleven steps to our door. My mother, no longer rebelling against the presence of this extra guest, would prepare his dinner, mixing whatever might be on our menu in Jim's dish. He, meanwhile, would encourage her by reaching up – he did not have to reach very far – and tugging at her dress, first at one side, then the other.

A favourite perch of his was the shiny brass fender which stood in front of our blackleaded fireplace. Here Jim would sit, his beak tucked into his glossy wing, until one of our visiting neighbourhood cats or dogs dared to enter in search of food or company. Instantly, the bird was transformed into a feathered fury as, wings extended and squawking ferociously, he would chase the intruder back into the street. It was, in fact, Jim's very vocality which led to his banishment. A close neighbour of ours was 'on nights' in one of the mills, then working at full pressure on wartime orders. He had to get what sleep he could during the daytime, and with Jim not far away, that was apparently very little. In those days, neighbourliness was the prime virtue. Sentence was passed and I knew there could be no appeal. Jim had to go.

I carried him back to the rookery where I had found him, perched him on a low branch and as I walked away, too quickly for him to follow, I knew how traitors feel. Did he adapt to life among the trees as readily as he had learned to live with us? I have often wondered. Or was he seen by the resident colony as an interloper and driven away? Had I been right or wrong to bring him home in the first place? One thing seems certain: if I'd left him there on the ground he would have become another of the fledgeling corpses you can find at the foot of rookery trees every spring.

It was a pity, though, that his brief sojourn with us inspired jealousy in some of the other lads living in Albert Street, who set about obtaining rooks of their own – with the aid of catapults.

10
A wicked place, Blackpool!

'THERE'S only one thing wrong with your mother,' Dad confided to me one day, with a strangely helpless expression on his usually placid face. 'She goes off t' deep end too soon!' He did not explain what had provoked this surprising and somehow disturbing complaint, and I was wise enough not to ask. Most of the time, my parents spoke with one voice and were apparently in complete agreement. There had been, of course, that Christmas morning when Dad and I had shared a sip of sherry at his brother Bill's house.

'There's no need to say owt about this to your mother,' he warned as we made our way home. As we both well knew, the first drink that led inescapably to ruin, was one of the things she was most anxious to protect her children from. She might well have written the old music hall song which warned of that single glass of champagne that 'led a poor girl into sin'. And there were other dangers, less visible, which impelled her to keep us where she could see us and worry miserably when she could not.

If I arrived home late from school, I would put my ear to the keyhole to listen for 't' wireless'. If it was 'on' I would quickly marshal my excuses and enter more or less boldly, for the ether-borne sound meant Dad was at home and the worst I could expect was a few sharp words (though rarely from him) of reprimand. If, however, the only sounds from within were of my mother at her housework, trepidation filled my soul; for her anger was quickly aroused and slow to abate. She seemed to be enraged by things other parents hardly noticed. But I know now that she could not help it: her contrition, when her fury had cooled, could be as hard to bear as her anger.

There was no sound from the wireless one day when I reached home even later than usual. I gulped, lifted the sneck gingerly, and fearfully pushed open the door. Had I been small enough I would have crawled underneath it. Desperately I searched my mind for some disarming topic to avert retribution.

'Where we goin' for us holidays this year?' I tried.

She never looked up from her ironing, nor did her expression change.

'There'll be no holidays this year,' she said, after a rather disturbing silence.

Could I believe my ears? Was it possible that I had brought such a dreadful fate on the whole family merely by coming home late from school? Dad's ten days holiday a year from his job on the buses was second only to Christmas as a time of sheer joy. Most of the families we knew never went away on holiday at all.

'Why?' I faltered in guilt and dismay. She didn't find it easy to explain, but at last the story emerged.

Coming off duty very late one night, Dad had placed the bag of fares he had taken that day in the accustomed place in the empty office and gone gratefully home. Next day, for no reason that he could guess, he had been called to 'The Office' and told that the money was missing. He had been incredulous. The slot, or whatever it was, through which the bag of money was always placed, should have rendered it utterly safe.

The management knew better than to accuse him – a more honest man surely never worked for them – but the money was missing, all twenty pounds of it, and in the company's eyes it was his responsibility. They had no choice but to deduct it from his wages until it had been repaid. I don't remember hearing him complain: he knew that a less trusted man would have been sacked on the spot.

But we knew we could expect an even more stringent time than usual and there would indeed be no money to spare for holidays. After the initial shock of disappointment I had my first experience of family unity and possibly gained half an inch or so in moral stature.

We talked long and seriously about how this barely credible disaster might have happened. Was it possible that someone lurking in the bus company offices had seen Dad deposit his takings and made off with what, in those days and conditions, amounted to a small fortune? Had he an enemy at the bus depot? That seemed incredible: everybody spoke warmly of 'Norman' – 'a reight good-livin' chap', as they would describe him to me on discovering who I was. My furious indignation on his behalf gradually cooled and as for the holiday, perhaps it wouldn't be so bad after all. We could go out 'for days', taking picnics perhaps. It wouldn't be the same as a week at Scarborough or Cleethorpes or Blackpool, but . . .

In these days when the whole world is virtually everybody's holiday oyster it is difficult to understand just what their few days' annual holiday meant to people who worked long hours for at least five-and-a-half days a week. Because my father had to take his holidays when it suited the company rather than his family, I had to make a special request to the headmaster to be excused school for that week. I always did so with complete confidence that the answer would be yes, and also with a slight sense of importance: here was just further evidence that our family was different – not only did we go away on holiday every year, but we did so at unexpected times while other folk were struggling out of bed every morning at the summons of the knocker-up or the mill's hooter.

The night before the holiday (for Dad always believed in having everything prepared in good time), our luggage, including buckets and spades and my teddy bear if I could smuggle him aboard), was piled ready in a corner of the room. The alarm clock would be duly and carefully set and, full of excited anticipation, we went to bed – early, of course, at my mother's insistence, since we would have to be up at the sort of hour at which Dad regularly rose for work when he was on 'early turn'.

Then, after a quick breakfast, speeded up by Dad's repeated reminders of the time, he would turn off the gas and the water (we had no electricity), pick up our luggage and emerge into the silent street, to walk to the bus or railway station, preferably the latter. Whether we travelled by bus or by train there was a good chance that either my mother or my sister, or both, would be travel-sick, though Dad and I never were.

The destination might be Scarborough, where we stayed with a gentle old soul called Mrs Downham, or Cleethorpes or more often Blackpool, where we were guests of a jolly, eternally smiling woman we knew as Auntie Maggie. Her two daughters, as extrovert as she was herself, would enliven the dining room with their salty chatter as they served the generous meals which were as much a factor in Auntie Maggie's success as her smile. For years the smell of bacon would awaken a holiday nostalgia in me, inducing visions of crowded sands, Blackpool Tower, sugary-smelling rock emporia and the sandy porch at Auntie Maggie's, where buckets and spades and toy boats awaited our pleasure on our next outing.

Inevitably the time came when the magic departed from holidays spent with parents. Naturally, my mother was reluctant to accept this developing independence, especially where my sister was concerned. Never as docile as I used to be, she was much more determined to defend what she saw as her right to go on holiday with the friends she worked with. It might not have been so frowned upon had they chosen anywhere but Blackpool.

'Blackpool's a wicked place,' declared my mother, as if she were talking of Sodom or Gomorrah.

Her face was all scrunched up as she spoke, as if she were trying to conceal behind her features the full dreadfulness she hinted at. I recognised the expression: it was the one she always wore when talking about things I was not supposed to hear.

'Why?' I said. They ignored me.

'Oh, *Mother*!' exploded Vera mingling pleading and exasperation in her tone, and proceeded to tell how many of her friends went on holiday unchaperoned without coming to the slightest harm.

I found it all very intriguing. Why should Blackpool be more wicked than anywhere else? Was Auntie Maggie wicked along with her irrepressible daughters? And if it were so wicked, why did we go there, once even in a big family party that included uncles, aunts and cousins. I knew, vaguely, that my mother was talking about something to do with sex, that mysterious atmosphere which somehow permeated the Blackpool air. It found expression in naughty postcards of busty bathing beauties, in near-the-knuckle jokes of concert party comics and in the glimpses of real-life girls who aroused feverish fantasies in small boys' minds by undressing in modest innocence behind towels on the beach.

Anyway, Vera got her way, as she so often did, and went off to Blackpool with her friends. She must have been eighteen then, the age at which her modern counterparts know all about seaside wickedness, though they probably learned it beneath warmer suns than Blackpool offers.

Sad to say, her holiday was short-lived. It was September 1939. During the week she and her friends were away, Dad tuned in our 'wireless' and we at home heard Neville Chamberlain declare in sombre tones that our country was at war.

Suddenly my sister's holiday was at an end. Blackpool, according to her recollections, virtually closed down immediately in an atmosphere of deepest gloom. A greater wickedness than this breezy, occasionally sleazy resort could offer was threatening to engulf Europe and neither brazen Blackpool nor Batley were to remain untouched by it.

On the very first night of the war the air raid siren wailed in Batley to Albert Street's huge indignation. The fact that Jerry couldn't wait to get at us was taken as proof that all we'd heard of German frightfulness was true. Air raid wardens ran about shouting 'Put that light out,' but were more or less ignored as officious jacks-in-office. Our neighbours gathered at their doors to discuss the matter, pausing only to listen to anything that sounded like an aircraft engine, and consider the views of self-styled experts on whether it was 'ours' or 'theirs'.

A middle-aged bachelor, a dignified Irishman, who had apparently rushed out to investigate before he'd had time to dress properly, was somewhat surprised by the presence of his neighbours. Hastily he tucked his shirt into his trousers, more fearful of ridicule than of the Luftwaffe. As it happened, Paddy needn't have risked embarrassment, because, to my great disappointment, Hitler left us in peace that night.

A little more than a year later, on 12 November, war really came to Batley. No-one worried when the sirens wailed their warning. We'd heard them so often before, uttering an empty threat, that they'd become almost a joke. Even the throb of aircraft engines left us unafraid – they were bound to be 'ours'. But our pulses beat a little faster when anti-aircraft guns sited on a neighbouring hill opened up, closely followed by a town centre battery. A soldier was killed when a high- explosive bomb detonated within a mile of Albert Street; a church was devastated and the home of friends flattened less than a minute after they had left for the shelter. An air raid warden now, with something more to do than shout 'Put that light out!', fell with a shrapnel wound in his leg as he yelled to others to 'Take cover!'

I don't remember being afraid. Probably I was still too young to accept the fact of my own mortality. People of my parents' age, after an initial shock of surprise that Batley, too, could find itself in the firing line, took it very much in their stride. Many of them, like my father, could well remember being under much deadlier fire in 't' last lot'.

When a fire bomb fell in a yard across the street, one large and elderly neighbour threaded her way amid the glowing debris, calmly sprinkling water from a saucepan. It took more than Hitler to cow the folk of Albert Street! We had no communal shelter to hide in, but our house at Albert Street, despite its peculiar construction, had a cellar, and there we sat during most of that noisy night, while candle-light threw shadows on the white-washed walls and my cousin Leonard, boon companion of my early years, who was staying with us, declared the experience to be 'the end to a perfect day'.

Another of my young contemporaries was among the St John Ambulance cadets who later, along with rescue workers, wardens and locally stationed soldiers, shepherded 'bombed-out' local folk to new quarters and fought warehouse fires, while a hazardous search began for unexploded bombs.

Since there was no obvious reason why little old Batley should have caught even such a moderate packet, the general opinion was that some of Hitler's navigators had gone off course and mistaken us for Sheffield or some other big arms manufacturing centre. The khaki cloth our mills were producing was hardly worth the attention we got on 12 November 1940. No doubt from that date we took the siren's undulating wail a little more seriously, and when Batley folk were asked to open their homes to child air raid refugees from devastated Hull, they did so all the more willingly.

11
It's ovver, lasses

O N the 11th of November, 1918, my mother, who had been keeping the home fires burning by weaving shoddy at Alexandra Mills on Bradford Road, Batley, had 'felled'. This meant that she had used up all the warp on her loom and, perhaps because of the time it would have taken to warp it up again, had 'laid away' and gone home for the rest of the day. Had she continued weaving along with her mates she would never have heard the hooters at eleven o' clock that morning, signalling to the town the news that 'the war to end war' had itself concluded at last.

She could hardly contain her joy, but she realised that in the noisy weaving shed she had left, her companions worked on, unaware of the joyful news that the slaughter which had bloodied the last four years was over. She just had to tell them! She hurried back to the mill, ran into the weaving shed and to the first of the weavers who greeted her with surprise, mouthing the words, 'Ah thought yer'd felled, Jinny,' she mouthed back: 'It's ovver, lasses, it's ovver!'

There was hardly a woman in that weaving shed whose family had not been robbed by war. From loom to loom the message was passed – 'It's ovver – it's ovver' – until the machinery droned away into silence and the cheering women flooded out through the mill gate on a tide of joy that carried my mother all the way back to Albert Street and home.

Her joy lasted until she saw the telegraph boy climbing the eleven stone steps to her door. Then it was replaced by terror – for her beloved Norman and for herself.

'Colbeck's?' asked the lad.

She nodded. The fear in her heart would not allow speech. Her hands trembled as she tore open the little envelope, and the words seemed to swim before her eyes.

'It *is* for Colbeck, in't it?' said the lad.

Yes, it was for Colbeck, but other Colbecks well known to her, who were soon to learn, on the very day the war had ended, that they had lost a son.

The lad held out his hand for the misdelivered telegram.

'Don't bother,' my mother said, her voice just audible, 'Ah'll tek it there meself.'

THE mill seems never to have been far from my family in times of joy or gladness. To celebrate my birth, my father's workmates at the mill had a 'fuddle', and one of my first jobs on leaving school was in the mill's 'finishin' 'oil'. Aunts and uncles were steeped in the mill's rich folklore with its laughter and tears. Yet to the world at large, mill life has become largely a comic cliché, based like many another cliché on a situation that never really existed either in fact or fiction.

Probably neither Thomas Armstrong nor Phyllis Bentley, much less J.B. Priestley, ever made a distraught character rush into the big house to stammer, as he twisted his cap in his hands, 'Ther's trubble at t' mill, Mr Mytholmroyd.'

Perhaps they should have said it more often and in earnest. Yorkshire folk are supposed to be tough nuts when it comes to industrial relations: that has certainly applied in the great Yorkshire coalfield where, in living memory, strikers have stood out almost to starvation point. Textile workers, at least to the best of my knowledge, have been a more long-suffering group or they might have been better paid.

There were no strikes during my brief sojourn in t' mill. But that was in the early 1940s when order books were full with demands for khaki cloth and army blankets. And anyway, the question 'Don't yer know ther's a war on?' must have seemed an unanswerable retort to any malcontent unreasonable enough to complain.

So the only trouble I came across in t' mill was usually of my own making. For some reason, not unconnected, I suppose, with my burgeoning adolescence, I briefly became a different person once I had entered the somewhat intimidating portals of Bottoms Mill (a name which described its valley floor situation, nothing to do with a certain Shakespearean weaver). It was not that I was brutalised by my surroundings or my companions, though occasionally one of my seniors might take it upon himself to cut me down to size. Perhaps I was compensating for the bullying I had put up with in my schooldays.

I passed through the mill's big, arched gateway with the feeling that I was entering a town, a fortress or a prison. It seemed huge and noisy, smelly and greasy and I wondered if I'd ever get out of it or was beginning a life sentence. At least I'd been warned about the tricks that might be played upon me. As it happened, though, nobody sent me in search of strap oil, a glass hammer or rubber nails.

The first job I was entrusted with was 'knotting'. I and another youth would stand side by side at a trestle table at the other side of which was a rolled 'piece' of cloth. How many yards it contained I never knew, being more familiar with its weight than its length. A grown man could carry one over his shoulder, though under-eighteens like me were not officially allowed to lift one single-handed. Generally speaking, in the finishing department where we worked, 'pieces' were moved about by two people, one at each end gripping the cloth in his hands. I can remember today how the thick khaki cloth tugged at my finger nails.

Standing side by side behind our table, my workmate and I would draw the cloth towards us, a yard or so at a time, and sweep its surface with our hands in a kind of breast-stroke motion, feeling for little knots in the cloth. These we would snip off with scissors, taking care (though often not enough, I'm certain) that we did not clip too close and make a hole. After a day or two of this my finger ends were pink and polished and slightly tender.

A more boring job it would be hard to imagine, but at least it offered the diversion of conversation, in my case with a youth of eighteen, a kind of head-boy of knotters, who, as my senior, was supposed to keep an eye on me. Meanwhile, Andra', the overseer, a gentle, anxious little man, kept an eye on him and me and all the rest of the department. It was because Andra' was one of our neighbours that I got the job, though I suspect it was not long before he regretted his neighbourliness. Anyone who knew me at all would have had no doubt that I was doomed to fail in such a job simply because I couldn't keep my mind on it.

Perhaps Andra' was reluctant to risk good relations in the street by taking me to task himself, and therefore relayed his complaints via my youthful guide and mentor, whose name I forget. He, in due course, informed me: 'Andra' says 'e wor watchin' yer yesterday an' yer wor just starin' rahnd instead o' feelin' for t' knots.' I remember feeling unreasonably aggrieved by this complaint, though in retrospect I'm sure Andra' was right and more knots escaped me than ever I clipped.

I could have explained that I was not really determined on a career in knotting but was only biding my time until my first successful book came out, but even I had more sense than to try that. No doubt Andra' was as relieved as I was when I got a job as messenger in the local railway goods office and handed in my notice. 'Ah well, it'll be more congenial there, more congenial,' he said. I wasn't quite sure what 'congenial' meant, but it sounded pleasant enough.

Work in the mill began at six-thirty or seven a.m. and at eight (or was it half-past?) the machines would stop with a whirring, running-down sound that to me was truly music. This joyous noise was immediately followed by a brief, echoing silence that was just as delightful. It heralded the breakfast break, when most of the men produced their sandwiches, but I, who lived not far away, rushed home for a precious half-hour away from the mill. Then it was back to the knotting and a tedium relieved only by the arrival of the 'weggin' – the wagon which brought 'pieces' from the neighbouring Hick Well mill to be 'finished'.

The wagon was a horse-drawn, four-wheeled, flat-topped cart in the charge of a short man, almost as broad as he was tall, with a voice out of all proportion to his size. If the running down of the machinery at meal times was my favourite sound, his stentorian shout of 'Weggin!' ran it a close second. Perhaps Albert, or whatever we called him, was the reincarnation of a Roman centurion of charioteers. Certainly I almost envied him the brief power that voice gave him to silence the machines and cause every man aged eighteen or over to hurry out into the mill yard to unload his wagon.

Being officially too young for such labours, I was free for fifteen minutes or so to sport and play with my fellow juveniles. At such times it was easier to forget the discontent that nagged at my soul like a toothache as I wondered what lay ahead for me. If the war went on long enough I would be called up, which to me at that age seemed an exciting enough prospect since I appreciated nothing of the terrors or tediums that war can really bring. Even air raids were momentary excitements then. Anyway, perhaps the war would end in a year or two – with victory for our side, of course – and then what sort of a life would be mine? Would it offer nothing other than the mill?

That prospect was unbearable. I wanted to travel, to be known for something of my own creation. Above all, I wanted freedom to live the life I chose. Meanwhile, I contrived to turn the hair of a good many estimable and well-meaning men prematurely grey as I entered their service and quickly destroyed their illusions that I was, in the words of the local parks superintendent, 'a likely-looking lad'. He was right, I looked likely enough and, to be fair to myself, I was as well-meaning as they were, but something inside me – call it ambition or just plain awk'ardness – always defeated my best endeavours.

Every night on my ancient Royal Barlock typewriter I tapped out poems, stories and articles, posted them to addresses culled from the *Writers' and Artists' Yearbook* and experienced the despair known to all but a fortunate few embryo scribblers as yet another large envelope flopped on the door-mat. Meanwhile, other boys I knew were getting jobs as junior reporters, though my youthful arrogance persuaded me that they couldn't be half as well qualified by nature for such a job as I was.

12
My affair
with Sarah

I HAD followed an undistinguished career in a variety of jobs before I 'entered journalism', as the rather grand phrase had it, shortly before I was sixteen. Doggedly I had sent contributions to the *Batley News*, where they apparently sank without trace. However, there were two local weeklies in Batley then, and a boy we knew, who had 'been to t' Grammar School', got a job on the *Batley Reporter*. From that moment I pined to emulate him, though for some reason I chose to offer the *News* my services.

Having finished my day's toil as a railway messenger, or whatever, on Thursday evenings when they put the paper 'to bed' I would walk the short distance from my home to the News office, a three-storey erstwhile rag warehouse, its facade adorned with sculptured heads of legendary monarchs, and politely request an interview with the Editor, Mr Roberts. This small town legend, whose myth survives strongly to this day, was usually 'tied up'. I would have to come back some other time, they told me. If it ever occurred to me that I was getting the brush-off, it made no difference. Finally, as usually happens in such cases, persistence paid off.

Rayner Roberts (referred to by all, including the man himself, as 'RR') is worth a book to himself. Purple of countenance, with a great hook of a nose constantly elevated towards the heavens, he was the proprietor of a group of local weeklies in what used to be called the 'Heavy Woollen District'. This area had its capital in Dewsbury, then a soot-black town whose fortunes were built largely on 'shoddy'.

RR took his newspapers and himself with immense seriousness and gloried, with some justification, in his reputation as first mentor to a clutch of successful journalists of the pre-war era. They included such as Harold Keeble, later to become a Fleet Street editor, and Don Iddon, a star correspondent of one of the national dailies. Perhaps RR found in their success some compensation for his own comparatively lowly niche in the press pantheon.

But if such were the case, only the more discerning suspected it, for his whole manner and lifestyle seemed calculated to project the image of a succesful 'self-made' man. He lived in Upper Batley, the posh part of town, and was a locally prominent Freemason, who bought and sold Masonic regalia from the office. While 'firewatching' – for this was wartime – my fellow juniors and I used to don the ceremonial aprons and fight mock duels with the swords.

In my memory, if not in fact, he drove to work in a Rolls. Did he really have a chauffeur? Somebody, I seem to remember, drove the car while RR sat in the back dressed like a millionaire, his derby hat just visible over the newspaper he studied so earnestly on his short journey from home to office. I do remember that the first employee aware of RR's arrival, as he swept majestically into the office yard, would whistle 'See the conquering hero come', and anyone in earshot of this chorus from Handel's *Judas Maccabæus* would immediately join in. Where else but in a staunchly Nonconformist area would such a warning be so universally understood?

Anyone failing to hear this alarm would certainly know that RR had arrived when the great man reached the top of the stairs which led to the floor where the Linotype machines, the reporters and RR himself had their being. There he would pause for a moment, presumably to recover his breath, before bellowing 'BOY', whereupon the nearest hapless youth would rush to do his bidding.

If ever a cliché were justified it was the oft-repeated saying that RR's bark was worse than his bite. With a bark like his, he had no need to bite, but whatever his failings, those who worked under him were at the very least intrigued, if not fascinated. The stories about him were legion. One of his much imitated idiosyncrasies was the punctuation of his sentences with the phrase 'There's-the-er'. It was frequently remarked that although the 'er' was always *there*, no-one had ever discovered precisely what it was!

Derrick Boothroyd, whose novel *Value for Money* was based on the Batley rag trade (nothing whatever to do with fashion), started his journalistic life on our competing paper, the *Batley Reporter*, as an 'articled pupil'. An apter term, he has suggested, might have been underpaid labourer. Rayner Roberts, recalled Boothroyd, in a special edition marking the centenary of the *Batley News* in 1979, was regarded in the *Reporter* office as 'a dastardly fellow', not least because he carried a large enough staff of reporters to cover every single funeral within our main circulation area.

Rayner's reasoning, frequently pumped into our youthful heads, was that 'names sell papers', a sentiment the *Reporter* staff saw demonstrated to their dismay in the two papers' contrasting circulations: in Batley, where RR had his HQ, the *Reporter* was definitely the poor relation, whereas in Dewsbury, where its own head office was sited, the *Reporter* was unquestionably king.

For some reason it fell to my lot to become cemetery correspondent, though without that title and certainly with no increase in pay. Every morning I would call at the cemetery superintendent's office and make notes of all the 'interments' due to take place within the next few days. These I would duly report back to the office, usually to find that I had been granted the doubtful honour of 'covering' the sombre ceremonies myself.

That is how I came to learn the entire Anglican funeral service as well as smatterings of other obsequies, ranging from Roman Catholic to what we would now call charismatic, which proceedings were sometimes enlivened with impromptu graveside choruses.

Just inside the cemetery gates I would await the cortege of taxis – only the well-off in Batley had their own cars at that time. Once the mourners had disembarked I would attach myself to the rear of the procession and start collecting the mourners' names as they walked towards the grave, relying on those immediately behind the 'family' to identify the closest relatives for me. The whole performance might be seen today as an unpardonable intrusion but I was constantly surprised by the tolerance of the mourners, many of whom obviously saw our interest as a sign of sympathy and respect for the deceased.

If the procession were not too long and my list was more or less complete by the time we reached the graveside, I would stand at a respectful distance, checking my notes while the parson intoned, 'Man that is born of a woman hath but a short time to live and is full of misery . . .' There were certainly rainy days in the cemetery when I must have considered those mournful sentiments no exaggeration at all, yet I never ceased to congratulate myself on my luck in having at least a toe on the journalistic ladder.

Unlike Derrick Boothroyd, I was never glorified with the title 'articled pupil', though I was as much a general labourer in RR's vineyard as anyone was in the *Reporter's*. When that stentorian shout of 'Boy' detonated on my eardrums it could mean fetching RR's afternoon coffee and buns from the confectioner's across the road ('No sticky ones, there's-the-er'), or filling the battery of fountain pens that nested in his breast pocket and wiping each nib carefully with a rag.

But as often as not, I was required to 'hold copy', which meant reading aloud everything from 'In Memoriam' notices to Town Council reports, while RR followed the text on galley proofs, correcting errors with flourishes of his impressive pens. The proof could be a full column in length, made up of every kind of local minutiae in no kind of order. As I tried to sort out the innumerable slips of copy, he would sit and fume until he could bear it no longer, then, with an irrepressible bellow of frustration, hurl the proof at me and fix his glare on some other victim.

Looking back, I can sympathise with the man. How on earth did he put up with me and my inflated idea of my capabilities? Perhaps he thought he saw some hidden talent lurking behind my illegible handwriting, or maybe, with so many young men already called up, he felt that enduring me was part of his personal 'war effort', along with publishing pictures and stories about 'Local Boys and Girls Called to the Colours'. In his office was a 'wireless', as we called it then, from which RR would glean the latest war news to enable him to bring a topical flavour to his 'Notes by the Way'. Thus, Batley lads and lasses all over the world knew that they and the war that kept them far from home were not forgotten.

I, too, as one of RR's 'old boys', had the honour of contributing to that *Batley News* centenary supplement (though not without visions of a ghostly RR scribbling irascible 'delete' marks all over my finer phrases). Re-reading my piece, I am hardly surprised to find that my contribution was largely concerned with my late editor and the human drama of our struggles to co-exist. I had joined the staff to be a reporter. Useless for RR to argue that he was training me to be something far better in his judgement, 'a newspaperman', apparently equipped with such rare abilities as tea-making, floor-sweeping, correcting type and anything else that might be called for.

We played a sort of cat and mouse game: when RR came into the office I usually contrived to be out on my 'district', gathering paragraphs about church meetings and club concerts or viewing corpses in the course of writing 'obits'. 'Would you like to see him?' a surviving relative would ask and you soon learned to accept the invitation in the spirit in which it was offered, just as you accepted invitations to tuck in to the funeral tea at the Co-op Café.

Funerals and obits and interminable cricket club meetings I could tolerate, for in their humble way they were the stuff of journalism. Not so my most hated task of all, acting as handmaiden to 'Sarah', the antiquated rotary press on which, week by week, the *Batley News* was printed. Sarah was doubtless so named because in those benighted, sexist days she was con-sidered to have the feminine temperament. She frequently broke down and it was widely believed that only one member of staff had it in his power to seduce the capricious old girl into any kind of response, let alone keep her going. Through no choice of my own I got to know Sarah very well, as, once a week, I sat in a kind of draughty well at one end of her gigantic frame to gather up the copies as she spawned a rapid, rattling progeny of papers.

I was as scared of RR as the next of his minions, but after one particu-larly draughty interlude with Sarah, including a series of break-downs that postponed my lunch beyond endurance, I told him this was no job for a budding journalist. And, to my amazement, he agreed! I was delighted. Not only had I won a moral victory over my tyrannical master but my true status had been recognised at last. For the rest of that day I stood at least six inches taller. Just one week later I returned to my normal size when RR banished me once more to the ground floor – and Sarah. I protested, of course. He looked at me earnestly. 'This is not an order, Maurice,' he said, meltingly. 'This is Rayner Roberts asking you, as a friend.' Back to Sarah I went without a murmur.

Such irritations apart, I revelled in producing 'specials', which offered me an opportunity to try my prentice hand at what I considered lively writing. Even the more prosaic golden weddings and eightieth birthdays (rare enough then to be considered newsworthy) were a source of joy to me, if not to my readers. But I was born too late for some of the riper characters encountered by the famous 'walking' writer John Hillaby, when he too sat at RR's feet. In *John Hillaby's Yorkshire* he recalls a spry old lady in black bombazine and jet whom he interviewed for the *News* on her 102nd birthday. After a pleasant chat, followed by tea and currant pasty, John was about to take his leave when she asked him, 'Don't you want to see my belly?' And when the startled young reporter, hardly believing his ears, investigated further, he learned that her belly bore scars from the chain harness she had worn as a young girl hauling coal tubs in the pit.

It may be that I was not of the right stuff to benefit by serving under Rayner Roberts. One man who undoubtedly was was Brendon Grimshaw, whom I first met when he joined RR's empire and half a lifetime later met again, to our mutual surprise, on an island in the Indian Ocean of which he was virtually king.

RR must have rejoiced to find in his hands such malleable clay from which to mould his ideal 'newspaperman'. Careless of whatever ambitions Brendon might at first have cherished, he applied himself diligently to whatever task was given him. Consequently, he was soon an expert Linotype operator and doubtless the possessor of many allied skills. They were to stand him in good stead, as I learned when we met on Moyenne, one of the most beautiful islands encircling the Bay of Victoria in the Seychelles Marine National Park.

The meeting was a complete surprise to both of us. Having disembarked from a cruise ship, I was climbing some rocky steps from a narrow strip of beach to an old Creole villa hiding among feathery palm fronds, when someone mentioned the name Grimshaw. The only owner of that name that I had known, other than Brendon himself, had been his father, a Dewsbury business man. Then, vaguely, I remembered a story which had circulated in Yorkshire journalistic circles that the ever-unpredictable Brendon was living on a 'desert island'. All at once, there he was before me, leaner, older, browner, but unmistakably the Grimshaw I had worked with more than forty years before.

After a fairly brief journalistic career in Yorkshire, Brendon, as I now recalled, had taken himself off to Africa, where he had had sole charge of some far-flung sheet. There, he had followed a sort of Kipling-esque existence, showing a masterly capacity to deal with his particular version of the White Man's Burden. Should, for instance, a rascally foreman try to pull the wool over Bwana Grimshaw's eyes, Bwana Grimshaw would demonstrate the impossibility of such an undertaking, plus his own dazzling ability to write, set and print the entire paper unaided. And all, as Brendon was the first to tell you, thanks to RR.

Precisely what prompted him to relinquish his role as RR's finest product, the perfect 'newspaperman', I cannot say. There is something of the 'old colonial' Englishman about Brendon, the type who, as my old teacher Hermon Hall never tired of telling us, was 'never at home unless he was abroad', for those were the days when we took Union Flags to school to celebrate Empire Day and learned by heart the lines of Sir Henry Newbolt's poem *Vita Lampada* –

The sand of the desert is sodden red, –
      Red with the wreck of a square that broke;
      The gatling's jammed and the colonel dead,
And the regiment blind with the dust and smoke.

There was nothing of the desert, however, about Moyenne, which Brendon bought and where he was living in more or less solitary state, with giant tortoises and birds and lizards and occasional parties of visiting tourists for company.

When two Yorkshiremen meet far from their native soil, it's invariably an occasion for celebration, especially if they happen to be old colleagues, who had lived within a mile or two of each other. And what did we talk about after a separation of forty years or so? What else but RR, described in all his ferocity by the extrovert Grimshaw to a bewildered Dutchman who shared our celebratory wine.

Had Brendon been a novelist rather that a newspaperman 'gone native', he would have found no end of material on his island, with its ghosts and graves of pirates and their undiscovered treasure reputedly worth £30m. Enough, as they might once have said in Batley, to put a rag merchant's will to shame – for as Brendon would agree, the riches of such Batley buccaneers were themselves of the stuff of legend.

Brendon was the last of only four of the island's owners to have actually lived on Moyenne in the last two centuries. I hesitate to call him eccentric but I don't think he would cavil at being called a character. He is in the tradition of the colourful journalists who used to enliven the local scene, like one who, even in Batley, sported an opera cloak while gathering material for his locally electrifying suburban exposés, with titles like 'Staincliffe with the Lid Off'. There was Jim Sheard, whom Boothroyd describes as a journalistic Beau Brummel in his check suit, bow tie and rakishly angled cloth cap. Also part of his public persona was a cigar, symbol of his comparative affluence due to his lucrative 'linage' earnings from local news stories sold to the dailies.

Another of that colourful breed that I remember, while forgetting his actual name, wore a wide-brimmed hat that might have won him a place in a cowboy movie. I suppose I was always rather a dull dog when it came to dress: for reporters a two-piece suit and a raincoat was 'rig of the day' (as we said in the Navy): no doubt it's a sign of advancing years, but I still prefer that to the scruffy jeans so often sported by the present journalistic generation, both male and female.

THE faraway years Brendon and I talked of on that tranquil island belonged to a different, far from peaceful age. And although Batley suffered nothing like the blitzing of London or even of Yorkshire cities such as Sheffield and Hull, we did not entirely escape the Luftwaffe.

From Albert Street, where we had experienced our brief baptism of fire, my family had moved to nearby Whitaker Street, where, on a patch of spare ground behind our house, Dad had erected our Anderson shelter, a kind of angular igloo of corrugated metal of the type issued to every family in Britain. It was sunk to about half its height in the ground and further fortified, according to instructions, with bags of earth. There was much discussion among our neighbours as to the efficacy of these structures and whether or not they would withstand a 'direct hit', a notion my father laughed to scorn. We would be much safer in the cellar, he said. And so, after a few draughty vigils in the shelter, whenever the siren wailed we either sought refuge below floors within the whitewashed walls or complacently waited in bed for the All Clear.

The war was the background to all our lives, but my generation seemed to pay it only scant attention. We assumed that 'our' side would win, but apart from that, we probably became bored with the conflict. Unless and until we were called up, it impinged little on our lives, or so we thought. Opinionated as any other youngsters we were far freer to speak our minds than our parents had been, and they did not hesitate to tell us so. We were known as teenagers, and we might have been forgiven for thinking we were the first of our breed.

Preachers and magistrates talked about 'Youth', as if we were a new and separate species, and praised or condemned us according to their mood. We belonged to Youth Groups, where we put on shows, for all the world as if we were part of a Mickey Rooney movie. And unlike our present-day equivalents we never complained that we had nothing to do. Or so it seems to me in retrospect.

We had grown up with the war and it didn't bother us unless it came too close. Even when the ship carrying one of my cousins was torpedoed it seemed only what you might expect to happen to someone in the Navy. He was rescued, so that was all right. I was saddened when another favourite cousin died in a prisoner of war camp, but quite untroubled by the possibility that at some future date a similar fate might befall me.

Our local papers published many news stories about people involved in one way or another with the war – killed, captured or missing. Once I was sent to visit a woman whose son had been reported 'missing, believed killed' months before, and was now found to be safe and well. She was sorry, she said, but she could not speak a word to me about what had happened or how she felt. Meanwhile, RR and I continued our uneasy relationship. But we were not always at odds.

One day on my rounds I found the local AFS (Auxiliary Fire Service) practising using a contrivance designed to rescue people from the upper storeys of bomb-damaged houses. It consisted chiefly, as I remember, of a tripod of poles from which a pulley could be run along a cable to the ground. It wasn't difficult to persuade the officer in charge to use me as their 'victim'. I was hauled to the top of the poles, from where I whizzed along the rope back to ground-level. Back at the office I wrote a highly dramatic account of my breath-taking exploit.

'I liked your story about there's-the-er firemen,' said RR when next we met, and handed me a ten shilling note. The firemen, too, I discovered, had enjoyed the glory briefly shed upon them, despite the fact that I had apparently exaggerated the height of the poles from which they'd rescued me. But no-one was complaining, certainly not me. Ten bob was ten bob in those days.

On the whole, life was fun, but I was conscious of a growing need for more space, both physically and mentally. Everything seemed too small – the town, my home, the paper and my job on it. I made a number of hopeless attempts to find a new post on a daily, but was still far too young to be considered for anything more than a copy-boy's job. So at the age of seventeen and three-quarters, the merest 'sprog', still too young by three months to qualify for my tot of rum, I announced my intention to join the Navy.

My mother, who had doubtless prayed earnestly that the war would be over before my time came, must have been terrified for me, yet she made no attempt to dissuade me. RR, in fact, made more fuss than she did. 'Nobody, there's-the-er, cares for poor RR,' he said when I told him my 'papers' had arrived. It was astonishing how guilty that man could make me feel.

Just a few weeks into my basic training at one of the Navy's 'stone frigates', a converted Butlin's camp called HMS *Royal Arthur*, a friend, also from Batley, handed me a cutting from the *Batley News*. It told me that RR was dead.

13
We joined
the Navy

'YOU must be daft, man!' said the big miner in the Irish Democratic League Club when I told him I had volunteered for the Navy. 'Go down t' pit, man,' he exhorted me, 'an' earn some brass!' How could I tell him that neither a 'reserved occupation' in the pit nor the big wages I might earn underground held any attraction for me.

At the time, Batley, on the edge of the Yorkshire coalfield, had enough working pits within its surrounding area to have something of a mining tradition, though it was essentially a textile town. No doubt the big miner, nurtured in that colliery tradition, could see no reason why anybody should not be proud to be a miner. I didn't tell him that one very strong reason for my volunteering for the Navy was to escape possible enlistment in the pit as a so-called 'Bevin Boy'. The name was derived from Ernest Bevin, Socialist and trade unionist to his backbone, who was Minister of Labour and National Service and therefore an apparently unlikely colleague of Winston Churchill in the wartime coalition government.

I suppose I was desperate for a change. In those days a young local reporter's life was spent between the clubs and courts, council chamber and cemetery. My father, I could sense, disapproved of my frequenting the clubs in search of news. He would have disapproved even more if he had met the club steward who later in another town apparently regarded it as his solemn duty to educate me in the varied resources of his bar.

To this club I would repair to write my copy after covering the local court. Proceedings finished around midday and I was then required to phone my copy through to head office so that it could catch the early afternoon edition. Phoning copy straight off my notebook never appealed to me. Apart from the inconvenience of holding the notebook in one hand and the telephone receiver in the other, it was a fruitful source of error. At the other end of the line the reporter or typist 'taking' the copy with headphones and seated in a little booth, might be keen to get out to lunch or to another job and not, therefore, in the most receptive frame of mind. Or, even worse, might be over-zealous.

'At Blanktown Borough Court today,' I might begin, 'Bertie Blenkinthorne was fined £30 for failing to keep a collie under proper control. He . . .'

'Keep a *what* under control?' interrupts my colleague at the other end of the line.

'A collie.'

'A *polly*?' (with growing interest). 'Do you mean a parrot? Sounds like a good story. Where's this Blenkinsop chap live?'

'Blenkin*thorne*. And it was a *collie,* not a —'

'I got the polly bit. What sort of a parrot, d'you know? African Grey, Blue-fronted Amazon? . . . Oh, Blenkin*thorpe*. I'm sure you said Blenkinsop. Is there an E on Blenkinthorpe?'

'Blenkin*thorne*. Just a minute, I'll check the final E. Have to put the phone down a minute.'

With the receiver dangling and an irate woman banging on the window of the phone box and mouthing her anxieties about her little Winifred who needs the doctor as she seems to be developing German measles, I flip through the pages of my notebook to see how I've spelt 'Blenkinthorne' in copying it from the court's charge sheet. I haul up the receiver only to find the line has gone dead.

How much more civilised it was to retire to an upstairs games room in the Blanktown Sports and Social Club, empty of members at this time of day, quietly write my copy, check the facts with my notebook, then peacefully descend to the lower regions and dictate my story on the borrowed club telephone, before becoming the subject of the steward's gracious hospitality.

It was from him that I learned the differences between old and mild ale and between Scotch and Irish whiskey. At my appearance he would run his eye along his shelves in search of something new for me to try. If any of my old Band of Hope mentors had been there it would surely have knocked them out quicker than a double brandy. They would have seen him as the embodiment of all the temptations they and my mother had warned me about from my earliest youth. Yet somehow I escaped the ruin she feared – at least, I think I did. If, as I left the club, I walked with a less steady gait than when I entered, nobody remarked upon it. And at least I was wise enough to telephone my reports *before* I embarked on my bibulous researches.

Reluctance to end up as a Bevin Boy was not by any means the major reason for my decision to join the Navy. I had the misguided notion that the Senior Service was a much more free and easy outfit than the army. But an even larger factor was my belief that travelling the world as a jolly tar, I would find endless scope for writing brilliant travel articles, perhaps even a book or two. The less desirable possibilities hardly entered my head.

'WAKEY, wakey, wakey! Rise and shine – the sun's burnin' yer bleedin' eyes out!'

Five forty-five in the morning and it seemed as if I had first heard that brutally hearty call hours ago through a haze of sleep as its perpetrator drew mercilessly nearer, rattling his stick along the line of holiday chalets.

'Take yer 'ands off yer cocks an' put 'em on yer socks,' chanted the seaman laureate at the top of his voice, and rattled the door hard enough to knock it off its hinges. This was not a dream, I realised. This was the Royal Navy, with its White Ensign at the masthead, its tots of rum, its grizzled old chief petty officers recalled from retirement to train lubbers like me, its passion for doing everything 'at the double', its Royal Marine bands, its gunner's mates, its unvarying profanity and – strangest of all to a landsman – its terminology.

Thus, although to all appearances I was lying in the upper bunk of a holiday chalet at a requisitioned Butlin's holiday camp at Skegness, I was nevertheless expected to entertain the illusion that I was 'in' (never 'on') one of His Majesty's ships, *Royal Arthur* by name, which by virtue of a kind of deliberate mass self-hypnosis was presumed to have all the appurtenances of a vessel of war. Even the guard parties were there to 'repel boarders' (a term some of the landladies of the town might have understood in a different sense). True, since this was Skegness, the bounding main was not really very far away, but that was quite irrelevant: the terminology would have been the same if we'd been moored in the heart of Leeds.

There was a 'quarterdeck' and a galley that produced food which the Norwegians and other foreign ratings sharing our 'ship' were more than willing to present to the younger and hungrier among us. And when the happy day dawned that I would be fortunate enough to leave HMS *Royal Arthur* to go in search of the fleshpots of Skeggie, I would line up to await a 'liberty boat' (disguised as a bus) that would take me 'ashore'. On the wall (bulkhead?) of the bus (boat) there would be a notice warning the libertymen against taking liberties with the conductress.

And as they travelled towards the bleak delights of wartime Skegness, the libertymen would sing – to the tune of *Dixie* I think –

We had to join,
We had to join,
We had to join Bill Butlin's Navy.
Ten bob a week
---- all to eat,

Bloody big blisters growin' on yer feet.
We had to join, etc.
If it wasn't for the war,
We'd be where we were before,
Butlin, you're barmy!

A weak last line, I used to think, since whoever was to blame for our situation, it certainly wasn't the future Sir Billy.

However, such 'run ashore' delights were still days away. Meanwhile we had to be kitted up, medically examined, punctured with needles, relieved of a tooth or two, graphically warned of the dangers of venereal disease and stuffed with all manner of indigestible information.

It seemed a year since I had said goodbye to my mother to embark (as the Navy might have put it) on a bus for Leeds *en route* for City Station and the train for Skegness. My date of departure had been 14 July, Bastille Day in France, which would have meant very little to her even had she been aware of it. What she did know, only too well, was that 14 July was also her birthday, and the fact that I, not yet eighteen, disappeared on that day with no guarantee when or even if I should return was what she might have called 'a funny sort of birthday present'. Not that she was noticeably laughing.

If she is now in Heaven – and I can't see her feeling at home anywhere else – I hope she will understand when I say that a great weight seemed to lift from my spirits when at last we had said goodbye at the bus stop and I set off into the unknown. I knew, almost with a sense of guilt, that she had no similar feeling of release. On that day, as she was to tell me later, the bottom dropped out of her world. How, I wondered, had I done it? How had I, who had not even been allowed to go camping with the cubs at Boston Spa or Saltburn, managed to break the bonds of maternal protection?

'Haven't *you* owt to say to him?' she had demanded of Dad when I first made it plain that I meant to volunteer (offering all sorts of spurious but confidently explained reasons that I thought might justify the outrageous idea).

'What can *I* say to him?' Dad replied. 'I volunteered meself.'

Reconstructing the scene in memory, I can see the look she gave him as a reward for such incomprehensible betrayal; for giving her an answer that was no answer at all. But if he looked at me, he must have seen gratitude in my eyes. I have long ago forgiven her for being over-protective, a 'fault' I am sure I shared when I, too, had children. Indeed, how to balance freedom and protection is the great dilemma of parents. She was no doubt equally protective of my sister, born five years before me and yet better equipped to take care of herself, perhaps because my arrival inevitably meant an increase of freedom for her.

With her own background and upbringing, my mother must have feared almost as much for my moral as for my physical welfare. Yet any anxieties she had were certainly not discussed openly, for sexual matters were rarely mentioned in the family. Having reached a certain age you were assumed, somehow, to 'know'. I later discovered that she considered my interest in animals must have given me some education in sexual matters. It was a reasonable enough conclusion, but animals were animals – your parents were something else entirely and in 'respectable' families at least, they appeared almost sexless to their children. Not until, feeling rather like a peeping Tom, I read the postcards Dad sent to Mother, and she to him, during the 1914-18 war did I realise how passionately they felt for each other.

There were cards printed in Paris with little silk pockets embroidered with the words 'To my dear Wife', all roses, with a card in the pocket reading, 'I don't forget you'. There were lithographs of soldiers standing bare-headed at wayside shrines. A card from him 'To Greet my Girlie' showed a soldier sitting on ammunition boxes writing a letter to the girl vignetted in the top left-hand corner. And from her to him, an almost identical card with the pictured roles reversed. On the back she had written, 'To MY hero'.

'To my heart's first love,' Dad wrote on one card. 'God bless and keep you for all time.' And on another, 'After I get home I shall never, never leave you again. I shall never go anywhere without you are with me. I shall tie myself to your apron strings with a knot that can't be untied'.

Passion was implied, rather than explicit. Desire was conveyed in veiled terms, as if – even between husband and wife – some things must not be expressed too openly. Card after card suggests, in the same code-like phrases, my father's longing to be told that his child had been conceived. Discreet references to 'news' from home and 'disappointments' make me understand how welcome the birth of my sister must have been to him in 1920, when he was back in civvy street and working in the mill. Constantly his words reveal a longing for home, but never a complaint, except about separation, or any sign of self-pity. Even the deaths in action of friends are recorded in sober but almost matter-of-fact terms.

Looking at Dad's battered Army paybook the other day, I find him described in an officer's letter, perhaps intended for potential employers, as 'a man keen on his work . . . intelligent, steady, worthy of every praise'. Just what sort of infantryman *was* my peace-loving father? Could he really, under the stress of battle, have imitated 'the action of the tiger' emblazoned on his York and Lancaster Regiment cap badge? One of his cards, written after returning to the front from one of his infrequent leaves, I find surprising: 'Everything is fairly quiet here now, but the lads say that we missed a treat. They say they enjoyed the sport immensely. We only lost a few so we didn't do bad at all.'

'Keen on his work... enjoyed the sport... we only lost a few...' All that suggests he was 'a good soldier', a marksman with, according to his paybook, the 'specialist qualification: Scout'. Among his medals is a gaudy-ribboned disc with a posturing angel on the obverse and, engraved on the reverse: The Great War for Civilisation 1914-1919. And there is one adorned with a laurel wreath and marked 'France 1917' which he apparently won as a dispatch runner in the '70th Infantry Brigade Competition'. Characteristically he had this fitted with a pin and chain for my mother to wear as a brooch, just as he had French coins made into bracelets for her.

I think the characteristic that I best remember of my father is the thoroughness that probably made him as good at soldiering as at anything else he turned his hand to. Intelligent, certainly, but in the best sense a simple man, he valued above all else his family and his peace of mind. Confront him with any abstract or unprofitable problem and he refused to 'bother his head' about it.

One day my sister, Vera, showed me a tiny crocheted baby's bonnet lined with silk that Dad had picked up in some shell-shattered house and brought home to be worn by his longed-for first-born. I wonder if the concern with progeniture, so apparent in his letters from the front, was born of the all-dominating awareness that he himself might not survive. And was it significant that he never filled in the page in his paybook provided for the writing of a will?

LIKE Dad, maybe, I took my survival for granted, so I did not make a will either. Not that I had any more to leave than he had, though according to a chaplain who gave us a talk during our early training, that did not really matter. Just *why* he thought we should make a will I cannot quite remember, which suggests that my ears were as deaf to his advice as those of my shipmates. I do remember the glazed eyes and wooden expressions that greeted his rather chirpy chat.

Warning us about the sins that might so easily beset us, he spoke about bad language and – not surprisingly – proved to be agin it. We might, he said, find ourselves sharing a billet with a fellow with 'a fruity tongue'. But not to worry, there was absolutely no reason why we should put up with the mental anguish caused by such ribald company. All we had to do was request a move to other quarters.

No doubt his intentions were of the best but I couldn't help thinking his advice rather unrealistic. I tried to picture the scene should anyone be unwise enough to act on it in any ship or naval shore establishment. Something like this, perhaps: having been marched before the commanding officer by a steely-eyed master-at-arms, the appellant stands to attention, cap under left arm, while the request is read out in a voice that would over-ride a storm in the Bay of Biscay:

'Ordinary Telegraphist Bloggs requests permission to move to a billet *not* occupied by a rating with a fruity tongue, SIR.'

Officer: 'Any idea what this man's talking about, Master-at-Arms?'

'No idea, sir.'

'Any idea what he means by a fruity tongue'?

'No sir.'

'What exactly *are* you complaining about, Bloggs?'

Bloggs, now yearning for a quick, painless death from heart failure, stumbles to explain.

'Swearin', sir. An' rude words an' dirty jokes an' that . . . sir.'

Officer: 'You know anything about this, Master-at-Arms?'

'Afraid not, sir.'

'Any of the men been swearing or telling dirty jokes? Anything of that nature?'

'Not to my knowledge, sir.'

'Request denied.'

Bloggs is double-marched from the office as the officer says, 'Better keep an eye on that chap, Master-at-Arms.'

Although my father would no more have made a Bloggs-type request than he would have jumped from the tower of York Minster, I never once heard him 'swear'. Instead of damning, he 'dashed' or 'blamed it'; nor did he verbally consign anyone to hell or threaten to go there himself, but usually to some lesser-known location called 'hummer' (though in extreme cases he might threaten to 'go to pot').

Once, on his day off from the local bus company, he called at the depot, perhaps for a brief union meeting, but left me outside because there would be 'language' used that he preferred I should not hear. I remember wondering – I was about eleven then – what sort of language this might be and how it could possibly be more lurid than that I heard every day at school.

I am now slightly less fastidious in speech than he was, but at heart I would still endorse his views, despite all the scorn fashion might pour upon them. The fact that our Anglo-Saxon forebears used 'four-letter words' in everyday speech, as plain, accurate descriptions, seems to me no possible argument for using the same words as ridiculous expletives. 'Prick' might be a perfectly good name for the male organ, even if the Victorians preferred something less descriptive; but the penis can hardly be noted for stupidity (or intelligence either, for that matter), so who but a moron would call a stupid man a penis?

Or was I just a prig? With hindsight I can recognise the youthful puritan in myself. As a child I had learned to see 'swearing' as one of the deadly sins, on a par with lying, drinking, gambling and yielding to temptation in any form, but particularly in the female form. Thus, while I was basically as lustful as most of my contemporaries, I had no time for casual fornication. A comrade and I once effortlessly acquired a couple of pretty young things outside Cookham Camp, near Chatham, provoking, as we walked them down the road, the applause and advice of our mates who watched like envious zoo animals from inside the high perimeter fence.

I was more than content to leave our conquests at the gate and return with virtue unsullied to my Nissen hut, but my mate fumed at what he saw as a golden opportunity gone to waste (the girls were none too pleased either!). With all the eloquence of youthful libido denied, he pointed out in agonised tones how easily we could have 'got 'em in those woods' and had our way.

Yorkshiremen are rarely mistaken for Don Juan, and I remained unmoved. It wasn't the judgement of God I dreaded so much as my mother's unstaunchable mortification should she have found herself with an illegitimate grandchild (though doubtless she would soon have learned to love it). Perhaps because he came from somewhere in Surrey, instead of the West Riding of Yorkshire, my mate had a mother who would not feel humiliated beyond bearing in such a case. Or perhaps he had a mother just like mine. At any rate, I knew that whatever the lost delights of the woods, they just weren't worth the risk.

The chaplain who sought to protect us from the 'fruity-tongued' would have seen no threat in me. With my upbringing it was easier for me *not* to cuss than to cuss. Others, lacking my Yorkshire immune system, assumed the prevailing local colour as effortlessly as any chameleon. One of these was a 'supply' rating, whose innocuous-looking 'fore-an'-aft' rig of peaked cap, jacket and collar and tie, seemed perfectly suited to his temperament. A milder character never drew a salty breath, and apparently he came from the sort of southern suburban home you would expect to produce such a model of quiet conformity.

The story soon got around of what happened on his first weekend leave. With decorous joy the family welcomed home the wanderer, who arrived just in time for tea in the parlour, with the best china on parade and an honour guard of fond aunts for admiring company.

As usual, he had little to say. 'Tea all right, dear?' asked his doting mum.

With his memories all too fresh of the supposedly bromide-adulterated brew that he would never learn to love, he was quick to reassure her.

'A ------' sight better than we get there,' he declared with rare feeling. The rest, as they say, was silence.

LADS thrown together from all parts of the country ribbed each other unmercifully about their origins. The Scots, the Welsh, the northerners, the Londoners were all twitted at every opportunity and in most cases learned to put up with it or retaliate in kind. Once, when a skinny Lancastrian and a burly Taff insisted that their grievance went too deep to be patched up without violence, a time-honoured solution was invoked. When the Captain of Marines had failed to convince the two that 'they ought to have more bloody sense', he called for the gloves to be produced and they met in the ring.

The result, as the rest of us had predicted, was a foregone conclusion. The Taff emerged victorious and more boastful than ever, though his pride was as nothing to that of the lad from Bury, smiling beatifically beneath a gloriously black eye. I'm sure he was prouder of that than he would have been of victory.

But Lancastrians had no monopoly of boastfulness. Though I risk being staked out on Ilkley Moor for saying so, when a Yorkshireman brags (though he might call it plain speaking) he can be pretty unbearable; which might, at least partly, explain why we are not among the best-loved inhabitants of the earth. The cockneys may or may not be brash and braggarts, the Scots dour and mean, the Taffs sly and unreliable, but the Yorkies... With them you paid your penny and you took your choice. We are all things to all men, called whatever you like, though it's rarely anything complimentary.

There are exceptions, but they are mostly found among folk who have come to know us well at close quarters and have been usually (and rather unflatteringly) surprised by the virtues we apparently strive to disguise as vices. Going back from leave, one blacked-out, doodle-bugged night, I sat in a railway station tea bar beside a 'civvy' – a cockney at that – who knew by my accent exactly where I came from and cherished the fondest memories of a time he had spent in my native town. With sincerity, if not originality, he described the back-to-back houses there as 'little palaces' whose black-leaded kitchen ranges gleamed in the firelight with a warmth matched only in the hearts of those who sat before them.

Cliché, of course, and from a Cockney at that, but it must have opened my eyes to a truth about my Yorkshire homeland that I had never seen so clearly before. Or why should I remember it after nearly fifty years?

So whence come the calumnies on our breed? It's no easy question to answer, but one example of the way we insist on bringing vilification upon ourselves could well be that supposedly humorous blot on our escutcheon called *The Yorkshireman's Advice to his Son*:

Hear all, see all, say nowt.
Sup all, eyt all, pay nowt.
An' if tha ivver does owt for nowt,
Allus do it for thisen.

It's no wonder, if we insist on presenting ourselves in these terms, that the rest of the world believes us. Or at best, not being blessed with the peculiar

Yorkshire sense of humour, is inclined to consider us rather more prone to folly than most. This was brought home to me while 'square-bashing' very early in my service life. In such a situation anyone, once in a while, can turn left instead of right or be lost in a moment of reverie when called to attention. But the old chief petty officer who was drilling us had no doubt where the trouble lay in my particular case.

'You from Yorkshire?' he enquired laconically. And with a degree of unison not always evident in their drill, thirty ratings replied with one joyful voice: 'Yes, Chief, he is!'

14
Goin' foreign

ENTERING Chatham Barracks for the first time was something akin
to walking into my first woollen mill. I felt immediately disoriented
by the size of the place with its parade ground, its great bare-
windowed barrack blocks, its endless bugle calls and broadcast announce-
ments, always quaintly prefaced by the purely rhetorical 'D'you hear there?
D'you hear there?'

The American alternative preamble, 'Now hear this', which, thanks to
insidious Hollywood, everyone seems to know better than we know our
home-grown version, may be more direct and logical, but for me the British
call had a strangely antiquated charm, like so much else in the Navy of the
early 1940s. Those words had probably been hurled against force eight
gales by means of simple voice-trumpets at a time when the only other aid
to ship-board communication was a pair of leather lungs.

If ever a service worshipped the past, it was the Royal Navy. The old
wooden man-of-war figure-heads encountered at every turn, like ghosts of
slain sea dogs staring in fierce disbelief at the modern version of the force
once commanded by Nelson and Collingwood, embodied this love of the
past. Scorn it, resist it though you might, it caught you up in an almost
reluctant pride that you belonged to something so drunk on tradition – a
draught even more potent than the rum ceremonially served each morning
after the call 'Up spirits'.

No Pharisee could have devised a more all-embracing code of observance for its own sake, so easily transgressed by, for instance, calling a
ship a boat, or saying you were 'on' instead of 'in' a ship, or calling a
ladder 'stairs', saying you were going 'out' instead of 'ashore', calling the
lavatories anything but 'the heads', or acknowledging an order with 'yes'
instead of 'aye, aye'. Just as heinous was entering a mess with your
cap on, or walking across the parade ground when you were required

to 'double', for despite all appearances to the contrary it was really the quarterdeck.

And woe betide you if you didn't stand to attention at sunset for 'Colours' when the flag was being lowered. This was the occasion for an ardent communist from Lancashire to feel greatly daring as he surreptitiously whistled *The Red Flag* – just loud enough for him to be heard above the obligatory silence but not identified.

I found life in the Navy a strange blend of toughness and romanticism. Squads of stiff-armed 'defaulters' holding rifles above their heads and unseasonably wearing tropical uniforms of white duck (in case they tried to go 'adrift') 'doubled' in formation up and down the parade ground. During this punishment (abandoned now, I believe) they prided themselves on never letting their pain or weariness show. 'Don't let the bastards grind you down' was the lower deck maxim most observed by 'skates' and scallywags.

At Chatham Barracks, as an air raid precaution in those war-torn days, we slept in specially excavated tunnels, having slung our hammocks on hooks in the wall. Sanitation was a communal bucket. What a relief it was to be moved to Cookham Camp nearby, an arrangement of Nissen huts in the middle of a wood. I don't remember air raid shelters there, though we were optimistically armed against air attack with a small gun mounted, I seem to remember, on the roof of the guardhouse. Having been given my nightly duty as a member of the gun's crew, I and my colleagues were briefly instructed in our duties by the rather elderly rating in charge of the armoury.

Those gun crews may well have put up a spirited, if brief, defence against a strafing Messerschmidt but they were as useless as a bow and arrow against the V1s, flying bombs, doodlebugs (call them what you will) which were just then appearing in our southern skies. Standing on London railway platforms, waiting for a leave train, you would hear the dying motor splutter to a stop, then, for an eerie interval, wait for the explosion when the bomb fell – on what, you wondered, and on whom?

'Skers' (naval shorthand for 'whiskers') our armourer was called, in honour of his truly splendid beard (or 'set') surmounted by a sharply pointed waxed moustache. To our youthful eyes he seemed positively ancient, the Navy personified. During who knew how many years of sea-time he seemed to have acquired all manner of matelot skills, such as making suits (we never spoke of uniforms) – which were just the job if you wanted a really 'tiddly' (smart) set of 'number ones' to swank in when you went on leave.

He showed us how to load the gun, how to aim and fire it and told us what to do if it jammed. Since the most we'd had to do with guns had been tossing a rifle about on the parade ground, a few lessons on prayer might have been more of an insurance. As I walked back to my hut, I rather hoped we would not have an air raid after all – especially that night.

It was not really surprising that we showed little promise in gunnery. Cookham Camp was largely populated by what the Navy called communications ratings (who, incidentally, were not too popular with other branches because, in the main Chatham barracks, due to our supposed relative brightness, we were given the 'cushier' numbers). To each other we were 'bunting tossers' (signalmen) or 'sparkers' (wireless telegraphists) with a few coders thrown in.

For some reason I had been selected not merely as a Telegraphist but as a Telegraphist (S), the S standing for 'special'. We 'special' 'Tels' were trained in German and Japanese morse procedures and also in the Japanese morse alphabet which comprised, I think, seventy-six symbols including the standard British alphabet of twenty-six. Our job was to intercept enemy wireless messages and pick up brief signals from surfaced submarines and other craft whose position might then be pin-pointed by the D/F (direction finding) equipment and, if possible in the moments available, attacked.

We were considered expert in reading high-speed morse. You can either read morse, or you can't. 'It's like 'avin' an ear for music,' said our instructing petty officer. 'If you ain't got the ear, morse can drive you crackers.' I took to it with an ease that surprised me and much enjoyed exercising this new-found facility. I could have been drafted to a station in Britain, where I might have spent the rest of my war 'reading' German transmissions from occupied Europe, but I had joined the Navy to see rather more of the world than that, so I volunteered to 'go foreign'.

In no time at all, it seemed, I was called to the Regulating Office and told by the 'crusher' (regulating petty officer) that I was on a draft to HMS *Lanka*, a transit camp in what was then the crown colony known as Ceylon.

THEY gave us fried egg and baked beans for breakfast, then, shortly after midnight, we boarded a train for Liverpool. We had been issued with water-bottles, a rather imperial touch, I thought, but not really surprising in a Navy which reputedly still keeps cutlasses in its stores. And we were given special small white kitbags, 'steaming bags', a name which to my ears had a splendid seafaring ring. These contained our white tropical kit and all we would need on the voyage. Our big regular kitbags were to be stowed below decks in the troopship along with our own personal hammocks. We greatly lamented the latters' absence when we saw the hammocks, so-called, in which we were expected to sleep,in the trooper – inferior things we thought them, all right for army pongos or the RAF, but hardly worth the attention of seasoned, sea-going matelots.

These flimsy articles, we were certain, would never keep us afloat for ten seconds, let alone for the twenty-four hours a properly 'lashed-up' Navy hammock, with regulation bed and blanket, was said to do. But we made the most of instructing the pongos sharing our requisitioned P and O liner in the fine art of slinging the things. Despite our efforts, most of the 'brown jobs' seemed to give it up as a bad job anyway and simply laid their so-called hammocks out on the deck.

The furthest I had ever been out of England was Rhyl. I doubt if I had even sailed in a pleasure steamer at Scarborough. As we came in sight of our vessel as she loomed up from the Liverpool dockside, I thought I had never seen anything so big in my life.

We embarked with a great sense of adventure, carefully concealed of course. In 1944 Britain was still very much at war. D-Day was just behind us and, though the chance of air attack had probably dwindled, there was certainly the possibility of an encounter with a stray from one of Hitler's die-hard U-boat wolf packs. Not that this gave us a second's anxiety except perhaps in the rare moments when we might stand briefly alone on deck watching the moon silvering the dark rolling waters and wondering how things were at home – in Yorkshire or Surrey or Ayrshire.

At eighteen, you have little doubt about your immortality. The tin boxes containing survival rations of chocolate were, in our view, for immediate consumption: most of us wasted no time wondering if we might some day need them in a lifeboat. But having eaten them, with less pleasure than we had expected, we rather wished we'd saved them.

Our hidden excitement mounted as the convoy formed up at Greenock. There were so many ships with their grey destroyer escort. Strange sounds filled the air, like our own liner's 'whistle' (laughably inadequate name) which almost made me jump overboard from shock the first time I heard its thunderous reverberation behind me.

Life at sea after the first few days proved uneventful. A grey-headed yeoman of signals formed a class of mixed sparkers and bunting tossers and exercised the lot of us in the use of the Aldis lamp, an instrument we wireless ratings had never seen at close quarters before. We beat the signalmen hands down at reading the flashed messages, possibly because we were accustomed to receiving our morse code (albeit by the ear) at much greater speeds.

When the duty officer, a kilted Scottish pongo, visited us on his rounds, our yeoman gave the order, 'Class . . . class, *'shun!*' In regulation style we sat bolt upright and clasped our hands before us – all except the inevitable idiot who made the mistake of leaping to his feet. The army officer, politely ignoring the gaffe, congratulated us all warmly on our keenness.

I felt rather proud that, unlike the pongos, we were under the control of men accustomed to life at sea and imbued with the Navy's obsession to keep the men occupied at all costs; hence those time-hallowed naval commands once heard when a ship was becalmed and idleness threatened – 'Hands to make and mend' or, if there were something to celebrate, 'Hands to dance and skylark'. This complacency, however, predated the lifeboat drill, of which more anon.

Five weeks can seem an eternity when you are eighteen, and though no doubt many of those taking passage were much older than that, the lack of exercise and activity eventually took their toll on all. A luxury liner intended to take the rich and privileged on cruises that probably cost far more than many a working man earned in a year, our ship was certainly never built to carry so many.

Even before enteritis broke out, the lavatories were barely adequate. When the disease began to spread, the resultant squalor was disgusting. Incontinent, pain-racked men queued desperately to gain entry to WCs already occupied by those determined not to leave them until their latest excruciating spasm had passed. Some were driven to relieve themselves in the wash basins. It was hardly surprising that the problem quickly spread or that I became one of its many casualties.

After several days of acute abdominal pain I went to see the Medical Officer. 'It's only enteritis,' he said and ordered me to move to the sick bay. Only enteritis, was it? Well, he could have my share! Thus began what was easily the most enjoyable part of the trip as my bellyache and nausea slowly subsided. On the credit side I had a clean and comfortable bed, there was the luxury of adequate lavatory provision in the sick bay plus the companionship of fellow-sufferers and comparative freedom to do what and go where I liked.

Two of my fellow patients who joined the ship in the Suez area had become badly sunburned while travelling from their base via the desert. They were quite philosophical about the probability of being put on a charge for allowing themselves to get in that condition. But for me, life was much pleasanter, for the moment at least. Having consumed my bottle of mineral water, a sick bay perk normally allotted only to non-naval personnel, I would trot off to my old mess to renew acquaintance with my shipmates and claim my RN-only lime juice ration.

'Limers' was one of the privileges which, for all I know, has now gone the way of the rum long supplied to the Navy in gratitude for some largely forgotten feat or favour in the great days of empire.

Life at sea can have a rare simplicity – in the climate of Suez, that bottle of mineral water, followed by my lime juice ration, was one of the day's high moments. And as long as I was standing by my bed when the MO made his rounds I was as free as a man could be within the confines of a ship.

Every so often the monotony was broken by the arrival at a new port with the endless movement of launches, pilot cutters and dredgers; by day there were the bumboat salesmen offering their wares in baskets hauled up by means of strings to the crowded rails of the deck. Local urchins scrambled for coins, including those which had been secretly heated in the flame of someone's lighter. By night there were the mysterious, faintly glimmering lights and sometimes still fainter music from shores that had never felt our feet.

The memories of that first voyage remain vivid. Gibraltar, where I had my unforgettable first sight of the Rock; Port Said, hypnotically attractive as the so-called 'wickedest port in the world' (what price Blackpool now?); the Suez Canal, where the British troops stationed on its banks shouted to us to 'Get your knees brown!' And the native felaheen, Egyptian peasants, who presumably shouted things rather less polite.

On my nineteenth birthday we arrived at Bombay and crossed the hot stones of the dock to join an ancient vessel, purpose-built as a troopship which was reputed to have seen service in the Boer War. She was alive ('running wick', as we say in Yorkshire) with enormous cockroaches. While loading our baggage in a hold, a revolted Marine attacked them with his bayonet, cheered on by the watching throng.

OCEAN travel held no perils for me before the day we had lifeboat drill. First of all, a naval lieutenant, who might have been understudying for the role of Captain Bligh, harangued us furiously for some considerable time on which route each unit was to take when the alarm sounded: the Navy would proceed along this corridor, up that ladder and down the next, then turn right at point A, and left at point B, making a veritable tour of the ship before mustering on deck to perform a variety of manoeuvres which would take us finally to the boat deck. There we should fall in, contingent by contingent, 'Stand *still*!' and await further orders.

Meanwhile, the Army and the RAF would each be following their own routes. And all this was to be done at the double. Inevitably it all went wrong. The Army, doubling along in twos or threes, would find themselves confronted at some crucial juncture by the Navy, which couldn't retreat because advancing fast upon them from the rear was the Air Force.

No doubt my memory is running away with itself when it conjures pictures of an infuriated Lieutenant Bligh jumping on his cap and threatening to hang us all at the yardarm – but by gum he was cross! I had more than a suspicion that our mob had done their fair share in fouling things up and was far from amused by the gibes heaped joyfully upon us by the other services. I mean to say! If the Navy couldn't get their lifeboat drill right, what hope was there for them? The experience of many more years has convinced me that it was simply another example of sod's law in operation. Or if you're of a classical turn of mind you can blame it on *hubris*, the pride that goeth before a fall.

The old tub we had boarded at Bombay took us on a dreamlike journey around the south-western coast of India to Colombo, where I was to spend the best part of two years. For the first months I was afflicted by the bites of mosquitoes and bed bugs, which turned septic in the humid climate.

I did not know it at the time, but after a few months I would be eligible to go up-country to a leave camp, delightfully free from such pests, though you were quite likely to find bugs on the train. These charming beasts had the knack of secreting themselves in crevices of the seats, there to feast on the plump and naked thighs of shorts-clad passengers who were unaware of their presence until the bugs had finished their leisurely meal and were sleeping it off in some well-hidden corner of the carriage.

Such minor irritations apart, these expeditions now form the most joyous memories of my service life. Boarding the train at Colombo was in itself a riotous adventure, peopled with officious porters, and all the varied and vociferous oriental passengers. When at last the journey began, Ceylon – as it was called then – revealed itself in all its variety and beauty. To lads fresh from sedate, law-abiding England, the sight of a train apparently encrusted with a human covering of passengers, who sat on the roof or clung to every available inch of the carriage was as much fun as a Marx Brothers film.

Elephants being scrubbed by their mahouts as they lay in the rivers we crossed by bridges made us goggle at what we had hitherto seen only on the cinema screen. As the train climbed from the low-lying coast to the central mountains, we would glimpse landmarks recognisable from postage stamp pictures, such as Adam's Peak (7,352 ft), venerated by Hindus, Buddhists and Moslems alike because of a footprint-shaped declivity at the summit, which followers of each creed attribute to Buddha, Krishna or Adam, according to their beliefs.

Our destination was Diyatalawa, a little mountain village where the air had a crispness that was wonderfully reviving after Colombo. The little shops, open to what I remember as a single street, held all kinds of 'rabbits' (naval parlance for souvenirs), from the ubiquitous carved elephants to leopard-skin handbags, made to your personal requirements for mum or the girl you'd left behind in Blighty.

At the leave camp we lived in huts pleasantly different from our 'bandas' in Colombo, their roofs thatched with dried palm fronds which provided a perfect habitat for suicidal cockroaches which you found drowned in your mug next morning; and rats which gnawed away the buttons of the great-coat you had stowed safely away, as you thought until, far in the future, you boarded the draft ship for home. At night you lay on your bed watching the varied fauna travel fearlessly along the central beam of the hut.

In Diyatalawa, however, when the sun went down and the evening air was cool you could almost believe yourself in England. Visiting a services leave club not far from our camp one night, I found myself one of a group staring as if mesmerised at the glowing coals and flickering flames of an open fire. That was the sort of homely image most of us cherished and, during our bleaker moments, longed to see again. For me, however, stone streets shining wetly beneath a gas lamp's mellow light were the stuff home thoughts and dreams were mostly made on.

During the day, despite the presence of the hills, the many alien sights all around made it impossible for us to console our homesick spirits by pretending we were in Yorkshire, Wales or Scotland. And for all our youthful high spirits and optimism (and despite the conviction of some folk back home that we were living the life of Riley at the state's expense), we were occasionally homesick in a sentimental kind of way, though the company of so many of our fellow countrymen acted as a buffer against unduly morbid yearnings.

By day we roamed the hills among the tea plantations, enjoying the dry heat of the morning sun after the clammy humidity of Colombo, on one occasion skinny dipping in a crystalline swift-running stream, unaware that we were under observation from a party of cheerful tea-picking Tamil women. Or bathing at the foot of a waterfall and scrambling to return to the bank after spotting a long golden snake leisurely swimming across the deep circular pool. Or we might go sightseeing to some temple, eat in a local restaurant or talk to some voluble shopkeeper who, had not acquired the wheedling or (understandably) the sometimes hostile attitude to the white men they had been trained for generations to call 'master', though 'matiah' was the closest many of them could manage.

It was at Diyatalawa in August 1945 that I heard that the war with Japan was over. A few months before, London had gone wild in celebration of the Germans' surrender and we had consoled ourselves with the thought that the end of our war must surely follow soon, though the Japanese were seen as a fanatical enemy, reputed often to prefer death to capitulation. Then came news of the dropping of the atom bombs on Hiroshima and Nagasaki. Our supremo, Lord Mountbatten, who had once visited us in Colombo to tell us how important we were, had no sooner said the A-bombs would not make all that much difference to the outcome of the war than we heard of the Japanese surrender.

That morning, my friend Bernard, from Scarborough, no less determined a character than any Yorkshireman ought to be, had insisted, that, war or no war, he was going to make a cyclist of me. 'Anybody,' said Bernard, 'can ride a bike.' 'I can't,' I said, but he wouldn't listen. So we hired two ancient velocipedes and found a gentle grass-grown slope down which I was to career in starting my tuition. Bernard was patient as well as determined, but when I had fallen off for the fourth time he seemed to lose interest in my progress and turned his thoughts to more momentous matters.

'Just think,' he said, his words almost echoing in the morning stillness, 'at this moment there's peace all over the world.' In our innocence we actually believed it would stay that way.

15
Man in
a new suit

RATHER more than three unheroic years after boarding the 'stone frigate' *Royal Arthur* at Skegness, I presented myself at the *Batley News*, resplendent in my chalk-stripe grey demob suit, and placed my Resettlement Form firmly on the general manager's desk.

I realise now that I might have acted with more tact, but I was just gone twenty-one and in a hurry to 'get on with my life', as people say today. The Resettlement Form, devised to ensure that the ex-serviceman's old job was restored, was presented in order to leave him in no doubt that I was back and meant to stay. He regarded me without enthusiasm. 'You've not been to see us very often while you've been away,' he said with no apparent regret.

'I've been abroad for two years,' I said. I might have added, 'You don't get many forty-eight hour passes from the Far East,' but I restrained myself. He was clearly unimpressed by my explanation. Neither of us seemed eager to break the pause that followed. 'Go away and have your leave,' he said rather wearily. 'They've all had their leave. Then come and see me again an' we'll see what we can do.'

With hindsight I can sympathise with him. The men who had been working on the paper when war broke out, plus those who had replaced them, plus *their* replacements, were now trickling back, each armed with a Resettlement Form and somehow having to be found jobs and paid, all in the frosty post-war climate. And as he and I well knew, most of those ambitious youngsters would be up and away to greener pastures at the first opportunity. I knew I would.

While I was working on the somewhat unexciting local treadmill my evenings were spent in free-lancing for any possible (or even impossible) market, and in going out with Brenda.

It was from Dad I first learned of Brenda. In one of his occasional letters, written, no doubt at the insistence of my mother, she being the regular family correspondent, he had mentioned Brenda's performance in one of the chapel oratorios. 'She's a grand lass with a lovely voice but no edge on herself,' he wrote, using a Yorkshire expression I have not heard for years ('edge' meaning conceit). Anyway, Brenda sounded the sort of girl I'd like to see more of. I've been seeing more of her now for nearly fifty years.

To her I confided my hopes and ambitions and – dutifully smiling – the poor girl listened. On 28th February 1948 we met as usual as I was leaving the office. I know the date because it was on the copy of the *Daily Mirror* in her hand (a rather different production from the *Daily Mirror* of today). She opened it at the feature page and held it before me. There, though I could hardly believe it, was an article with my name beneath it. I have it in front of me now in an ancient cuttings book, labelled and dated in Brenda's neat hand. Suddenly Bradford Road, Batley, took on a roseate splendour – I had made the nationals!

'Let Rolling Stones Roll!' my article was called. Its doubtful thesis was that if your offspring tended to flit from job to job in early working life you shouldn't worry, because he or she would thereby gather invaluable experience and 'every stone must stop rolling sometime'. As I explained, before I was sixteen I'd had no fewer than six jobs, ending up as reporter on the local paper. If those five hundred words meant anything at all, they indicated that at least I had my fair share of the cheek required in the calling to which my rolling had finally brought me.

Whatever my other failings, I clearly did not lack industry. Leafing through my old cuttings book, even I find the range of themes impressive. There are facetious essays contributed to *Flash*, the Huddersfield Press Ball newspaper, under such titles as 'The Cockroach and I' (though I don't remember having ever read Kafka), 'Newts Don't get Fresh' ('fresh' being a West Riding synonym for 'tight' or 'sloshed') and 'Giants – and Refreshment of Same', in which I mused on what was meant by phrases like 'He arose like a giant refreshed'. What, precisely, I asked my readers, was the effect of refreshment on a giant? 'Is he more gigantic or does he just get fresher?'

At least my old chief sub, the adorable Bill Lowis. approved of these nonsensical trifles and with his customary vagueness expressed his conviction that these efforts would undoubtedly 'do me some good'. 'Where?' demanded my fellow subs with one voice.

Alongside these frivolities my cuttings include short stories I wrote for the *Sunday Companion*, an evangelical weekly subscribed to by Brenda's Grandma, and, with a fine ecumenical impartiality, a story with a Biblical theme for the *Mothers' Union Journal*. My naturalist tendencies are in evidence, too, with pieces on 'Making a Bird Sanctuary' and 'Ceylon's Giant Workers', based on my exceedingly slight acquaintance with elephants in Ceylon. Rather similar in origin was my 'Big Cats of the Far East'.

I may not have faced many ferocious felines in the wild, but at least I had taken home a leopard skin handbag from Ceylon (now Sri Lanka) for my mother. All of seventy rupees it cost me, cheap enough in all conscience, and my conscience was perfectly clear about it in those pre-conservation days. I had selected the required portion from a newly killed leopard's blood-stained pelt spread on the floor of a native shop while on leave 'up-country'. Less colourful, if more closely based on personal knowledge, was an article entitled 'My Friend Jim', describing the rook I found and kept as a pet until a night-working neighbour's complaints about its cawing led to its enforced removal.

For the *Boys' Magazine* I wrote 'Your Local Paper – Gateway to a Career', for the *Preacher's and Class Leader's Magazine* (I think it was) I wrote 'Faith and the Mind of a Child'. 'An Insect Aquarium' in *Water Life and Aquaria World* described a cabinet for small aquatic creatures in the construction of which pickle jars ('preferably of the square variety') were utilised.

Held together with a rusty paper clip, there are reviews from teaching magazines of one of my first books, a highly improbable children's adventure story, published by E. J. Arnold and Son, for whom I worked as an assistant editor when I could no longer tolerate the endless weddings, funerals, courts and council meetings of the local round.

Chapter I, An Enemy Unknown, begins: 'Jim Mayhew looked up, amazement on his face. "No wonder we're running short of petrol! Look at this,"' he exclaimed.

'Alan Benton, his nephew, and Dick Evans, Alan's friend, jumped down from the truck. Uncle Jim, as both boys called him, was examining a small hole in the petrol tank, which was leaking freely.

'"What caused that, Uncle Jim?"' asked Alan.

'"Looks like a bullet-hole to me," was the puzzled reply."'

The teaching press received it kindly. 'Witch doctors, ivory thieves, lost aeroplanes, a tribal rebellion and a madman, surely sufficient action to satisfy our liveliest schoolboys,' admitted *Teacher's World and Schoolmistress*. 'Thrills enough in a Dick Barton profusion in Africa . . . well told,' commented *Education Today*.

LOOKING back (a phrase I find it increasingly necessary to avoid) I realise that my ambition was in itself something of a handicap. The longer I endured the local treadmill, the more boring I found it and the less I appreciated the creative opportunities my work really presented.

Not that originality and flair were much encouraged on many of the local weeklies of those days. A good shorthand note, an ability to get names right and the knack of keeping on the right side of local councillors, vicars and cemetery superintendents (in none of which I excelled) were surer pathways to appreciation. I certainly worked at my Pitman's shorthand. While still only fifteen I attended a few evening classes, but apart from striking up a brief friendship with a female student, the course proved unproductive.

She was the only girl I had ever known called Sadie and no doubt the name itself was part of the attraction. It had a racy ring to my ears, though Sadie by any other name would have seemed as sweet. She had a pleasant, smiling face, a head of shining blonde hair, and freckled legs. I mooned about her when I should have been mastering Sir Isaac's halving principle or practising my thick strokes and thin.

I gathered that she lived in Birstall, only a couple of miles away, famous as the birthplace of Joseph Priestley, the discoverer of oxygen, whose statue stands in the market place. But I had no thoughts of Joseph as I wandered Birstall's streets, only of Sadie with the golden hair and freckled legs. And, in the way miracles can happen to the young, we met! She was standing in the yard of the house where she lived (probably putting clothes on the line for her mother). We exchanged shy smiles and greetings before she told me she had to 'go in'.

In retrospect I wonder if we had earlier made some vague, now forgotten tryst and whether, incredibly, she too was on the look-out for an encounter. If so, she gave no sign and nor did I. Girls rarely did in those days. That would have been considered 'forward'. No doubt Sadie, like another girl who sent me love letters (stonily ignored), when I was in Standard VII, is now long married and a grandmother. But how many less fortunate souls may have spent a lifetime of loneliness just 'because' (in the words of an old song beloved of Sunday school baritones) 'I were shy'? Songs seem to say it all. 'They try to tell us we're too young' could have been written in 1940; though they didn't just 'try'. When I was 'too young' they hammered the message home, chiefly because, for a girl, 'getting into trouble' was of all sins the most heinous; and being the male instrument of her misfortune ran it a close second.

Despite such frequent infatuations, my interest in the female of the species was mostly academic and sex more active in the imagination than the loins. It was something to dream about, as I dreamed about becoming a famous war correspondent, typing, grim-faced and shirt-sleeved, Clark Gable-style while all hell blew up around me. Michael Parkinson says that as a junior reporter on the *Barnsley Chronicle*, he equipped himself with a trench coat and a slouch hat in imitation of his idol Humphrey Bogart. But because, unlike Bogey, Parky ventured on his missions by push-bike, he had to anchor the hat with a piece of elastic under his chin.

Real journalistic opportunities were all too often missed, largely because there just wasn't enough time to reflect on their possibilities or to experiment in the writing. I remember, for instance, the 'spiritual healing' service I attended for one or other of my early papers in some West Riding town.

After prayers, a hymn and an address by the white-coated healer, sufferers with various crippling disabilities hobbled to the front of the hall, there to be egged on to perform various more or less painful exercises to the applause of the congregation. The more painful the exertions demanded by the spirits, the more enthusiastic became the congregation, whose appetite for cures, at no matter what cost to the afflicted, appeared insatiable.

One poor man, who had struggled on to the platform only with difficulty, was ordered to bend his arms behind his back. It was painful just to watch his efforts to do the impossible. But the healer was implacable; the poor man just wasn't trying, he said. Of *course* he could do it! 'I *can't*' said the sufferer, with streaming tears. But the healer was determined and the crowd were on his side. They demanded, they bayed for the sufferer to be healed so that their faith in the spirit world might be vindicated. They had no compassion for a sufferer so stubborn.

'Yer can tell 'e's soft just to look at 'im,' said a woman in the seat behind me, with blistering scorn. Unhesitatingly, her companion agreed. It was one of the occasions, sadly not too rare, when I have been ashamed of being human. Yet perhaps I too was all too human in my lack of charity: that poor, unthinking, unfeeling congregation wanted a sign to convince them of the reality of that happy land far, far away, since the land they lived in offered them so little.

I should have written it 'like it is' as they say today, fearlessly defying grammar. But that would have meant writing *two* stories – one for me and one for the Great God Spike, in whose honour too many of my finest efforts had already been impaled.

Cruising the Outer Hebrides by fishing boat.

Daughter Anne and friend Leo in Italy.

Brenda in Norway.

Thailand: friendly python, uncertain Brenda!
Opposite: Knighted!

" The Mark Twain Journal makes for very interesting reading." President Gerald R. Ford

"Mark Twain is the only American writer who is also an American hero, known to many men and women who have barely read his books. He created many characters but none of them is greater than himself."
Carl Van Doren to Cyril Clemens

$1.00 a copy   **CYRIL CLEMENS**   **$3.00 a subscription**
EDITOR
MARK TWAIN JOURNAL
Established 1936
KIRKWOOD, MISSOURI 63122

5 February 1979

Dear Maurice Colbeck

In recognition of your contribution to Modern Humor, you have been elected A Knight of Mark Twain.

Cyril Clemens

"I never miss a copy of the M. T. Journal." - William Faulkner

"Put me down ditto to the above statement." - Lyndon B. Johnson

"Cyril Clemens, a worthy kinsman of Mark Twain who brought light into all our lives."
John F. Kennedy

"I obtained my 'New Deal' slogan from Mark Twain's A Connecticut Yankee." President *Franklin D. Roosevelt, told Cyril Clemens upon receiving the Mark Twain Gold Medal at the White House, December 8, 1933.*

With fellow speakers Tim Sebastian (centre) and Barry Took (right)
at a Yorkshire Post *Literary Luncheon.*
*(*Yorkshire Post *picture by Joan Russell, of Asadour Guzelian agency.)*

At the launch of my book The Calendar Year *with (left) the book's photographer, Derry Brabbs, and (right) Richard Whiteley of Yorkshire Television. (*Yorkshire Life *photograph by Jack Ireland.)*

A joint book-signing session in York with my late lamented friend Harry East (seated), author of Laughter at the Wicket *and* Cricket is for Fun *(Whitethorn Press).*
*(*Yorkshire Life *photograph by Fred Spencer.)*

At Harlow Carr Gardens, Harrogate, with gardening writer Philip Swindells (left) to launch an exhibition of Yorkshire Life *flower paintings by Nancy Dyson.*
*(*Yorkshire Life *photograph by Asadour Guzelian.)*

Retirement portrait by Yorkshire Life *group camerman John Cocks.*

with best wishes.

Brian Tutt.

Do I look like that? A rather Mephistophelian caricature by an old bookseller friend.

16
Brenda and
her world

WHEN, in the first transports of young love, I was bidding Brenda prolonged goodnights in the semi-darkness of her hallway, Grandma would sometimes loom large upon us on her laborious pilgrimage to bed. 'Ee, Maurice,' she would pant as she mounted the first few stairs, 'yer can't be as fond o' yer bed as I am!'

Bed, it seemed, though she no longer had anyone to share it, was her favourite destination. Its tried and proven attractions were second only to the anticipated delights of 'the Farther Shore' for which, as she frequently assured us, she was shortly to set sail. Whenever she felt slighted or mis-understood, she would remind us of the imminence of her voyage. This did not necessarily have the desired effect; for in that largely female household, there was plain speaking on all sides, which came as quite a shock to me after the rather more restrained atmosphere of my own early home-life. In Brenda's home you were expected to know where you stood with the rest of the family without a great deal of sloppy reassurance. On the whole, perhaps, it was a healthy arrangement.

The one person who rarely engaged in verbal exchanges was Brenda's father, Harry, who seemed to exist in a sort of insulated masculine bubble unaffected by the arguments and emotional goings-on sparked off by the fact that his two daughters, his wife and his mother-in-law all lived together in the same house with the occasional aged aunt. Such birds of passage now and then found sanctuary with the family due to the fact that my mother-in-law's heart (though never worn on her sleeve) was of a size in keeping with the rest of her.

The house itself had been something of a culture-shock to me. A large stone terrace house, it appeared palatial compared with the two houses I had known. There was a baby grand piano in the room where we all opened our presents at Christmas – under a real Christmas tree, of course, and

where I would sit with the family on Sunday evenings in an atmosphere that
seemed relaxed and even luxurious.

But it was in the large workaday kitchen that I first met Harry as he was
taking his evening meal from the hands of Grandma. She was ever dutiful
in her ministrations to the man of the house – he-who-must-be-fed, as she
had been brought up to consider the dominant male – though if Harry held
that position he did so by tradition rather than by conquest, for he was
hardly a dominating character.

It was usually either Grandma or Mrs Marsden, the cleaner, who looked
after Harry's inner man when he came home from his work as chauffeur
for a Dewsbury textile family. Vera, Harry's wife and Brenda's mother,
returned home later from business: she was company secretary for a firm
in Heckmondwike founded by a Jewish immigrant. That immigrant's son,
Harry Weiss, was now Vera's employer as managing director of the company,
the business of which was carbonising. This was the process by which cotton
was removed from woollen rags which were to be reprocessed as reclaimed
wool and woven into shoddy cloth. But that was in the days when the Heavy
Woollen District was more than a mere name and when rag merchants'
astronomical wills were still among the most eagerly read contents of the
Batley News and *Reporter*.

Harry looked up from his tea as I entered. 'How d'ye do?' he said.
'How d'ye do?' I replied and though we were alone in the room, that was
the full extent of our conversation that first meeting. We never had a great
deal to say to each other, partly because I was no good at conversing on
either of his favourite topics, football (preferably Rugby League) and
motor-cars. The days were still far in the future when I would drive a car
myself, though I feel we did achieve a warmer rapport years later when he
took my first company car, a *Triumph Herald*, for a spin.

'It's fast!' he said as he disembarked on returning to his own gate.

'Don't be daft,' replied his wife, as if he had confessed to some kind of
weakness. It was almost an automatic response, for she was in many ways
the typical West Riding mother-figure brought up from birth to recognise
the mental frailty of the male sex in general and husbands in particular.
But in many other ways she was not typical. She was, for instance, the
main provider for the family and it was due to her that they lived in such
comparative style.

She was a woman of great presence and strength of character allied with
generosity. In their declining years, old aunts and uncles and parents found
refuge in her comfortable spacious house, which, despite her daily absence
on business and aided by the faithful Mrs Marsden, she maintained in
immaculate condition. Someone once described my mother-in-law as a ship
in full sail, a cliché, of course, but apt enough if the vessel you had in mind
was the sort entered in the Tall Ships Race. She had a rich soprano voice

and in her youth had been a star of the local amateur operatic scene. All in all, she was what would once have been called a fine figure of a woman. And she had a way of taking charge of things. It was she who largely taught me to drive. Despite the professional criticisms of her chauffeur-husband, she did it her way – as purposefully as she did most things, continuing at the wheel until she was past eighty.

Through her association with Harry Weiss she had close friends among the Jewish community of Leeds. They would often visit her hospitable home, sometimes talking about the sufferings of members of their families in Hitler's Germany. After my first press trip to Isreal they virtually queued to question me. They brought a continental colour and vitality to the West Riding scene and it may have been their influence that encouraged Vera to take Harry on continental holidays while most of the local population were still largely content to holiday at their beloved Scarborough. And yet she remained, in essence, as 'Yorkshire' a woman as ever I knew.

At the heart of this gynocratic realm, Harry followed his masculine existence with unruffled, quiet independence. He might occasionally make a half-hearted demand for peace and quiet in the middle of a family alter-cation, but nobody took the slightest notice and he was not in the least put out when the argument, whatever it was about, continued to swirl enjoyably around him as if he hardly existed.

If things ever got too much for him in this all-women world he could always escape to the local Conservative stronghold – the Blue Leet Club as it was called because of the blue lamp over the door. Here, Harry Barrowclough was not only highly respected but renowned as a wag – as, indeed, he was at home when the women had nothing more important to do than enjoy his mordant humour.

I don't think he approved of me as a potential son-in-law, whereas he approved highly of George as a suitor for Enid, his elder daughter. George, a product of the old-established Grammar School (which my son later attended) was then a future headmaster, whereas I, a mere journalist, followed a calling Harry neither understood nor respected – unless one happened to be a big-name sports reporter, like one renowned local product who wrote for the *Daily Express*. George, furthermore, was the son of sociable, extrovert parents with a great zest for life, who blended perfectly into Harry and Vera's ambience.

But if our relationship was not a warm one, Harry and I were never in open conflict. He did not exactly ignore me – he just did not take me into account. I wish now that I had made greater efforts to achieve a rapport with him, but perhaps that was not possible. He was a ripe character in his way, even if he shared some of the limitations of a Yorkshireman of his time.

My own parents, unlike George's, had little beyond their early background in common with Harry and Vera, though my mother, with her reliable instinct, saw through the differences and admired Brenda's mother for her ability and generosity. Mrs Barrowclough, she would say (somehow, they were never on first name terms), was the sort of woman who'd 'give her last shilling away'. Fortunately, she was also the sort of woman who would make sure she never got down to her last shilling, though I could believe that more than once, in her leaner times, my own mother did.

Like our parents, Brenda and I had different views and attitudes. Advisers on what used to be called romance in the sedate magazines of yesterday often insisted that to have any hope of success in marriage, husband and wife should 'laugh at the same jokes'. Brenda and I rarely laugh at the same jokes. Instead, we laugh at each other laughing at the jokes we separately find hilarious. Thus, like a true Yorkshire couple always ready for a bargain, we reap a double benefit! However, if we don't always find the same jokes amusing, we do occasionally find ourselves shedding harmonious tears; and that, I believe, may reveal an even closer affinity. It is highly unlikely that I shall ever set up as a marital 'counsellor' (to use a word tiresomely in vogue), but if I do, the first question I shall ask my clients might well be, 'Can you cry together?'

Whether marriage will still be in vogue when that day dawns is about as problematical as whether Brenda will ever read this book, since we no more read the same books than we laugh at the same jokes. But if she is not among my most avid readers (except incidentally via the word processor), she has always been my most loyal supporter and frankest critic. This may well stem from the tradition of plain speaking which runs in her family, and since a more Yorkshire trait than that you will never find, I ought to be able to cope with it. Perhaps it goes hand-in-hand with the common sense which is surely one of the least-valued virtues in the often pretentious world of today.

Did those magazine marital advisers also suggest that opposites attract? If so, they were probably right. At any rate, after more than forty years of marriage we two, though certainly opposites in temperament, are still together and will no doubt stay that way. We are opposites, for instance, in our capacity for worry, or rather in the fact that she has very little capacity for worry, while I can worry for no better reason than that I can't quite remember what I ought to be worrying about.

But there are debits and credits in all human activities. Those who never allow themselves to worry never know the full joy of hearing the long awaited step in the hall as the delayed one returns at last; never know the joy of finding the missing letter, which was under their noses all the time and which is usually discovered, without fuss, by some quiet, methodical Brenda, who keeps her head when all about her are losing theirs and no doubt blaming it on her. A natural problem-solver, she has given many years to the Citizens Advice movement, displaying a surprising degree of passionate determination in fighting for the rights of many often ill-equipped through circumstances to fight for themselves.

We rarely quarrel, but when we do it is usually my fault, the odd harsh word having being provoked precisely because Brenda is always so maddeningly calm. Yet how often have I been grateful for that unshakable equanimity. 'Nichevo!' as my dear old chief sub, Bill Lowis, used to say, making the most of his only word of Russian – 'Not to worry!' My advice would be: worry if you must – but for goodness' sake don't worry about it!

But I owe more to Brenda than relief from stress (and a son and a daughter) I owe evenings of opera at the Grand Theatre, Leeds, a form of music that had been rather alien to my family, for whom 'good music' was chiefly oratorio. Through Brenda I was easily enlisted in all manner of musical enterprises. Once, when she was singing Antonia in a local production of Offenbach's *The Tales of Hoffman*, I found myself assisting the chorus whilst out of sight behind the rather shaky scenery that I happened to be supporting at the time – and feeling myself to be a hero unsung, if not unsinging.

If I have a rival for her affections it is indeed singing, which has been and remains a great part of her life, involving her in membership of three choirs at once, with problematical conflicts of loyalty if two of the choirs (with differing uniforms, of course) happen to be competing in the same musical festival. Such situations might defeat a less resourceful woman, but not Brenda, who refuses to recognise a problem even though she's married to one.

That loyalty of hers could well be inherited from her mother, whose ferocity in defending her own put me in mind of a lioness with her cubs. This quality surfaced with a vengeance after I had been made president of the Henpecked Club, though I had only joined that amusing brotherhood to write about them. Mother-in-law, unfortunately, found it a little difficult to see the joke. I can only hope that she has forgiven me at last.

Parenthood has pains and pleasures hardly suspected by those who have not experienced them. Brenda, with her usual equanimity, never doubted that her first child would be a girl. We called her Anne. 'Anne!' exclaimed Grandma in disgust. 'Plain Anne!' Her own rather dated taste was for more flamboyant labels. Four years later we had a son, again as 'ordered' by Brenda, and named him Peter. 'Peter?' protested mother-in-law. 'That's the sort of name you give to your dog!' Neither of my offspring, I am happy to say seems to have suffered from these handicaps.

17
Gone to the bad

IT was, I am told, Gertie Roberts, daughter of RR himself, who remarked, on hearing that I had got a job with E.J. Arnold, the Leeds educational publisher: 'He'd never have made a reporter.' As daughter of that great mentor of newspapermen, she may well have prefaced the remark with the well-worn words 'Father says'. In any case it dented my ego not one jot, firstly because I was recklessly indifferent in those days to other people's opinions of me, secondly because I didn't want to 'make a reporter' anyway. Certainly not the sort Gertie would have valued.

This is not to say I held such in contempt. On the contrary, I marvelled at their unflagging dedication to the minutiae of local politics, their industry and their diplomacy in coping with self-important councillors and touchy town clerks. I just could not share the enthusiasm that enabled them to put up with the irritations and limitations of local weekly life.

My new appointment, humble though it was, created something of a stir in local newspaper circles. Two applicants were finally appointed to fill the single vacancy, since Arnolds' editor was unable to decide between us. The other successful (or semi-successful?) candidate was my old schoolmate Kenneth Cassidy. Obviously better suited than I to the local weekly scene, Ken finally gained his heart's desire by becoming editor of the weekly *Brighouse Echo*. Having gone to school together we were on friendly terms, despite the fact that before our joint appointment he was working on our competitor, the *Batley Reporter*.

In those days, competing really meant competing, even to the point of trying to outrun our rivals – to for example – the home of a couple celebrating their diamond wedding, on the off-chance of snatching photographs of the happy pair before the 'opposition', as RR invariably called them, beat us to it.

The picture was the thing that mattered. Any junior worth his salt could almost have written the interview without even seeing the venerable pair. 'Asked for their recipe for a happy marriage, Mrs Bloggs said, "Always pull together and forgive and forget".' After sixty years her husband, in the manner of many West Riding men, said little: he was possibly too well trained either to agree or differ.

At one point during my career with the *News*, the picture war with the *Reporter* became so intense, after some trifling dispute, that RR declared total war on the 'opposition' by ordering his leg-men to seize every single photograph on every story. 'I'll make their lives a little hell!' he said. He may or may not have deserved his reputation as a great journalist, but by gum, what an actor!

I wish I could record that following this decree, processions of reporters were to be seen en route to the *Batley News* office weighed down with snatched family photo albums. Alas, RR's picture-grabbing edict was conveniently forgotten almost as soon as it was pronounced. He had satisfied his instinct for the dramatic and his soul was soothed.

Starting work at E.J. Arnold's was in some ways like going back to school. Nursery rhyme pictures adorned the editorial office walls and all the editors and most of the authors were teachers or lecturers. There was something of a Dickensian air about this place, where the clerks sat on high stools, and, as Ken and I pretended in juvenile mockery, wielded quill pens. If you arrived late for work a 'late slip' was passed to the head of your department. Since Ken and I each had to undertake a laborious bus journey to get to Leeds for half-past eight, we collected more late slips than most.

I fear that some of those worthy clerks saw us as rogues and vagabonds who had unaccountably fallen on our feet. Not only had we got a job with Arnold's, we'd got two jobs when there was only one on offer. And in Editorial at that, where everybody knew you were paid astronomical wages for lounging about all day in an office of your own, just reading things.

We certainly did read a lot of things, both in manuscript and proof, including the latest titles in the series on which the fortunes of E.J. Arnold were reputedly founded. Known as B.S.Rs in the office, *Bright Story Readers* to the world at large, they were the pride and joy of the oldest working director, whose name I forget, but who was said to be in his eighties. Perhaps he actually initiated the series. At any rate, when it became known that B.S.Rs were used in Armley Gaol, Leeds, to help prisoners improve their powers of literacy, he seemed to take it as a personal compliment.

Ken and I must have been a great disappointment to Arnold's editor, who had so rashly persuaded the company to hire the two of us. For Ken left after about a year and I followed him out some six months later. It was nobody's fault. We were simply not suited by age, background or temperament to a job where the deadlines were so widely spaced. Having read and reported on a manuscript, we would edit it, if it was accepted, and send it to the works for setting.

Months would pass and then, suddenly, a set of galley proofs (presenting the text, undivided, as yet, into pages) would appear. By this time we had almost forgotten what the book was about. Having painstakingly read and corrected the 'galleys', we would send them off again to the compositors. After what seemed a great interval the work would reappear as page proofs to be read and corrected yet again.

Eventually, with mingled excitement and dread, we held in our hands the completed book. The trepidation was caused by the fact that the main destination of these books was schools, and schools contained teachers. They, of all people in the world (explained the editor), were most likely to write and complain that 'Hereward' had been spelt 'Hereword' on page forty-one, line three. There it would regrettably remain to corrupt the spelling of the youth of England until, in the hands, perhaps of their grandchildren, the book parted from its covers.

It could be argued, insincerely, that we felt this was too heavy a responsibility, but the simple truth is that we were bored. Hence we both took ourselves off to join newspapers, though at the time I had my interview for a job on the reporting staff of the *Huddersfield Daily Examiner*, I had for some reason firmly resolved not to take it. I had, in fact, only presented myself at their office in Ramsden Street out of mingled curiosity and politeness and was uneasily aware that I had not had the best of shaves that morning. The one or two people who interviewed me could not have been more charming.

I may not be offering the best advice to young interviewees if I tell them to decide in advance that the very last thing they want is the job on offer. However, it seemed to work for me. When, to my surprise, a letter arrived offering me the post, I somehow felt morally obliged to accept it. At Arnold's my notice was accepted almost with incredulity. I was even summoned to the managing director's office and politely asked to explain my behaviour. I had the impression that hitherto nobody had ever left Arnold's until old age or death had made their continued employment impossible.

By present-day standards they were, perhaps, an old-fashioned firm, but during my short stay there I saw no reason to doubt that they deserved their good reputation. It was rather singular that in joining the *Examiner*, a stoutly Liberal organ with ads on the front page in the manner of the old *Manchester Guardian* and a resounding motto at its masthead – I was exchanging one old-fashioned humanitarian employer for another. Both of them are enshrined in my memory as models of their kind and I wish there were more of that kind about today.

On the morning I joined the *Examiner*, the chief reporter, a permanently worried, incurably conscientious and very well-meaning paragon, told me that there had been so many applications for the job I'd been given that letters to the unsuccessful had actually been set in type and printed. No photocopiers in those days, I suppose. Or if there were, the *Examiner* hadn't caught up with them.

IT should be part of every young Yorkshireman's education to work in Huddersfield, so much the quintessential West Riding town that if it were a human being it might be accused of over-acting.

For one thing, it became famous as 'the town that bought itself'. Much-quoted to newcomers, that tag dates from 1920, the year Huddersfield Corporation bought the Ramsden estate, including most of the town centre, from Sir John Frecheville Ramsden, sixth baronet. Having once acquired itself, Huddersfield was fully entitled to benefit from the considerable profits accruing therefrom. And Huddersfield had always an eye to profit.

Perhaps because profit and property are taken seriously in Huddersfield, they give rise to some of the town's best stories. Like this one: a Huddersfield man with plenty of brass coveted a piece of his neighbour's ground, but for all his wealth was having difficulty getting it. Time and again he upped his offers, but all to no avail. At last, in desperation, he almost begged: 'If Ah cover t' ground wi' *gold sovereigns* will you sell?'

Did a flicker of interest light up the land-owner's stony visage? Of course not. Huddersfield men display flickers of interest nobbut sparingly and then only in extreme emergency. But at last the hesitant vendor took his pipe from his mouth. Perhaps ten minutes elapsed before he spoke. Then, 'Ah'll tell thi what Ah'll do,' he said (and Huddersfield men don't promise that lightly). 'Ah'll accept thi offer – '

Before the other, with a glad smile, could seize his hand, the reluctant vendor raised it to warn against unseemly haste. 'Ah said, Ah'll accept thi offer to cover t' land wi' sovereigns. But think on, Ah want 'em liggin' on their edges.'

The *Examiner*, though it flourishes still, represents the kind of small provincial daily that has largely vanished even from Yorkshire – certainly in the form I knew. Its scholarly, bow tie-wearing editor, Elliot Dodds, was a Liberal of the old school. His leaders were penned in stately prose as befitted the kind of minor *Manchester Guardian* he edited.

Perhaps it was the *Guardian's* adoption of front page news that influenced the *Examiner* to follow suit. At any rate, I well remember the first night the paper appeared with its front page innocent of ads but emblazoned with, of all things, news! Oh, the anguished thought that must have gone into the planning of that front page! The big question was: 'How will the readers take it?' And not without reason, for many of the *Examiner's* readers were under the distinct impression that they not only owned the paper (whether or not they advertised in it or even bought it) but that they had every right to dictate its policy.

Hence the phone call that reached me that night in the sub-editors' room, whence all but I had fled (presumably to the *Examiner's* favoured pub, the *Albert*). The caller was a reader, who, despite my protestations of innocence, congratulated me warmly and personally on our new front page as if I alone were not only responsible for it but had wrought the transformation just for him.

I was to spend four entertaining years in that subs' room as one of the devoted minions of one of the funniest and most likeable men I have known. He was W. G. (Bill) Lowis, the chief sub-editor, who proved to me, once and for all, that a man can be not only a legend in his lifetime, but also a source of mirth, an authoritative executive and a much-loved colleague.

Bill's first action every morning on entering the subs' room was to fling his cap at a hook on the wall. Usually it perched there to the applause of the assembled 'table' of subs. Occasionally, however, it fell forlornly to the floor to the accompaniment of groans. It seemed to me that Bill's cap was a barometer of the sort of office weather that would prevail that day. If it fell we could expect the worst: if it stayed put, the staff were heartened to tackle the day's disasters and frustrations with good humour and optimism.

These frustrations – and I am sure they are the sort that cause premature grey hairs in all newspaper offices – included, for a time, a strange ban from on high on use of the word 'man' (and presumably 'woman') in headlines. This was possibly relaxed, though I cannot remember with certainty, in the case of any 'man' who had been convicted of murder or possibly of riding a bicycle without lights. But until such a one had been found guilty, he must be courteously given the title 'Mr'.

Advancing years allow me to sympathise to some extent with such apparently timorous inhibitions, though young 'publish-and-be-damned' enthusiasts like us, who never worried that a 'man' might cancel his advertising if labelled with such scant civility, found them almost insupportable. 'Man' was such an easy word to get into a headline and that was all we cared about.

Bill, I felt, shared our frustrations, for he was one of us. Returning from the morning conference with galley proofs streaming behind him and in no mood to throw his cap at anything, he would mumble something about having 'lost another battle', slump into his chair and glower at his assembled crew who smiled sweetly in response.

Suddenly, 'Nichevo!' he would exclaim and fling himself into preparing the next edition. We all knew, because he'd told us, that the word was Russian and meant 'Not to worry'. If ever a single word expressed a man's entire philosophy it was this. Bill delighted in collecting words that amused him and played with them as happily as a kitten with a ball of wool. His conversation was larded with phrases like 'man and boy', 'in and among' or any malapropism some wiseacre from the comps might enliven the day with as he held forth on life in general and the failings of sub-editors in particular. What a pity Bill did not live into the era of *glasnost* and *peristroika*!

I don't know if it was Bill who nicknamed one of the main tribal celebrations in the Huddersfield calendar, 'The Mrs Blunderland'. If he didn't, it was only because someone else during the hundred and some years of the event's existence beat him to it. Lasting a week, this musical marathon with its umpteen classes and almost innumerable contestants, could hardly have had its birth anywhere but in the home of the world-famous Huddersfield Choral Society.

The competition's real name was not Mrs Blunderland, of course, but the Mrs Sunderland Musical Competition. Nightly the progress of the various hopefuls was recorded in the *Examiner*, and with the fortunes of so many entrants in so many classes to be chronicled in print small enough to tax the eyes and concentration of the most assiduous proof-reader, how could the occasional howler be avoided?

Everyone in Huddersfield knew all about Mrs Sunderland. Born humble Susan Sykes in nearby Brighouse, she was received by Queen Victoria, who, after autographing Susan's copy of Handel's *Messiah*, remarked with monumental condescension: 'I am Queen of England, but you are Queen of Song!' That, at least, is the story, but as the meeting of queens took place in about 1858, I am unable to vouch for the actual words of either. Being a Briggus lass, Susan might well have said, 'Aye, well I'm right suited, but yer needn't have bothered'. For Briggus folk are not easily over-awed.

Born in 1819, Susan began her musical life at the age of twelve when the choirmaster at Brighouse Parish Church, Luke Settle, heard her singing as he worked at his anvil and was captivated by the beauty of her voice. Luke, surely the original harmonious blacksmith, went to see Susan's parents and offered to give her singing lessons at his smithy. The legend that, as he taught her, he beat time on his anvil may be apocryphal, but if true, it surely provides a classic example of a thrifty Yorkshireman performing two jobs at once.

But to be fair, if Luke were no more mercenary than Susan, he probably taught her for nothing. Her first professional fee was five shillings (25p) which must have embarrassed her almost as much as 'the terrible flunkeys' she met when she was commanded to sing at Buckingham Palace. She'd seen nowt like them in Huddersfield, nor ever wanted to.

It is not recorded that Susan walked from Brighouse to London, but I'd hardly be surprised to learn that she did. No matter what the weather, every Sunday morning, when she was singing in the choir of Huddersfield Parish Church, she would walk a round twenty miles to and from her

Brighouse home, and when she was singing oratorio in Leeds she would trudge a total of thirty miles.

It was at Leeds, during the opening of the city's splendiferous Town Hall, that the Queen of England and her consort, first heard the singing of the Queen of Song. 'We mun have that lass down to t' Palace, Albert lad,' said the Queen (or words to that effect). The rest, as they might well say in Huddersfield, is history – and the Mrs Sunderland Musical Competition.

18
Some of
my yesterdays

I BECAME a collector of cuttings the day the first ill-advised editor published some of my early vapourings. I would certainly have found it more profitable to collect stamps, yet some of those clippings are now invaluable in their way, and probably better than any diary in shedding light on the person I used to be.

I don't preserve my personal cuttings in a book any more. Perhaps I'm too lazy. Nowadays I either lose them or, if they seem worth keeping, I stuff them somewhere for the time being and then, like a squirrel with its nuts, forget where I put them. The cuttings I acquired during my office days were better looked after, partly because they might be needed, and unquestionably because they were dealt with by one or other of the secretaries who put up with my vagaries over the years.

Most durable of these was Jean Paget, who must surely have been something of a masochist: for having once escaped my absent-minded tyranny, she returned after an interval (during which she acquired a husband), and, in all, was my secretary for some seventeen years – that is a good deal longer, incidentally, than many marriages last today.

Jean, an archetypal Yorkshire lass from Yeadon, was the most devoted dog-lover I ever knew. That characteristic might seem irrelevant in a secretary; I mention it largely because she demonstrated at least two of the most admirable of canine qualities: not only was she the perfect guard dog, protecting me infallibly from publicity-seeking pests and cranks of all varieties, but at the same time she acted as a first-rate retriever.

I never actually issued the instruction, 'Find, Jean!' I simply told her what was lost and she simply found it. Jean, among her other Yorkshire traits, was not averse to a good argument, but to continue the canine metaphor, her bark (on the rare occasions when I heard it) was unquestionably worse than her bite. If, in a future life, human beings can return as animals, Jean surely deserves to come back as a dog. I can only hope she takes that as the compliment it is meant to be.

The oldest and inevitably scruffiest of my cuttings books contains proofs of advertisements for special features in *Yorkshire Life*. Composed by me with my copy-writer's hat at a rakish angle, they declared, for instance, 'Sleepy Hollow is Waking Up!'. Sleepy Hollow was and remains a nickname for Goole, though how it earned such a title I cannot imagine. A product of the Victorian age, Goole is still the only port in the West Riding (a geographic title I refuse to surrender no matter what the bureaucrats say), and no less of a port for that.

If you intend to write your 'life' but don't trust your memory, hoard your cuttings, but if you write books you hardly need a memory at all – or so I almost concluded when I turned up this passage about Goole which appears in my book *Yorkshire* (Batsford, 1976). It describes an experience of which I have only the haziest recollection, but which at least conjures up the Goole I could hardly have remembered so vividly without it:

'Touring Goole docks as I did recently in a tug, I found it almost impossible to believe that it was fifty miles from the sea . . . Cornelius Vermuyden, whose genius brought the port and town to birth, would surely have thrilled if he could have stood beside me in the tug's wheelhouse on a wet and blustery morning when the wind added white-capped waves to the surface of the water. Busily we chugged from basin to basin, passing ships from ports like Trondheim, Bilbao, Tromso, Hamburg, Bremen. "That one's bound for the Shetland Isles with coal," said my guide, a man in a felt hat, who suddenly gave three furious blasts on his siren as a suicidal tender cut across our bows . . .'

Precisely why I was privileged to tour Goole docks in a tug I have no idea. Not that it matters. But Cornelius Vermuyden deserves to be more fully introduced to those who don't know him. He's remembered well enough in Goole as a brilliant Dutch engineer, who, in the time of Charles I, drained and tamed the wild and lawless fenland of Hatfield Chase and cut his arrow-straight Dutch River across the flatland from the overloaded River Don to the Ouse at Goole.

Another advertisement proof among my cuttings takes us from Goole to Pontefract: 'Black Town with a Heart' announces the ad – 'six pages of pictures and comment in the February issue of *Yorkshire Life*. 2/– from all newsagents'. Today the magazine costs £1.50 and is considered by many to be cheap at that. The description of Pontefract as a black town would hardly, perhaps, be so appropriate today. The adjective referred to Pontefract's associations with coal and liquorice, neither of which plays as big a part in the life of this grand old town as it did in bygone years.

To the eyes of strangers, that word 'black' might have had a different and less fortunate connotation. I am by no means the most chauvinistic of

Yorkshiremen, but I must admit to a wistful sense of regret that towns like Pontefract, with their associations with industries such as mining, are so readily dismissed as boring or ugly by a type of folk from further south whose invincible ignorance we can only try to forgive. I could sometimes almost curse William Blake for his line about 'dark, Satanic mills' which is so often mistakenly dragged into their ill-informed, prejudiced and self-opinionated diatribes.

Our monthly 'town features' so revived the flagging circulation of *Yorkshire Life* that they were quickly copied by other regional magazines both inside and outside our own group. In principle there was nothing new about the idea of featuring a town in several pages of words and pictures, but hitherto it had been done only once or twice a year and to my eyes, at least, the articles were often fairly yawn-provoking, written reluctantly at the behest of the advertisement department who needed 'something to sell off'.

Among the more sensitive directors there was a school of thought which held that there was something rather vulgar about 'featuring' in words and photographs people who would never in a millenium have graced the pages of *Who's Who*. But when it became apparent that you could sell from five hundred to a thousand extra copies on the strength of one such article, even the former doubters agreed that the practice had its merits. And after all, as I'd always insisted, towns were where people lived; towns had character and characters, folk and folklore, and there was always a controversy sizzling away somewhere if you took the trouble to look for it: usually it hit you in the eye as soon as you entered the place, picked up the local paper or spoke to an inhabitant. And if there wasn't a worthwhile controversy you could always poke a little friendly fun at the place.

To judge by the newspaper advertisements yellowing in my cuttings book, Yorkshire in the sixties was in a continual state of ferment. NORTHALLERTON – ONE-WAY STREET OR BATTLEGROUND? *Residents speak out*... HANDS OFF THE STRAY! (This time, it was the turn of Harrogate folk to speak out)... THE BATTLE FOR BARNSLEY... KEIGHLEY WITH THE LID OFF... And, lest anyone should accuse us of sensationalism, I would occasionally give the soft pedal a gentle touch with something like TEMPERATE TADCASTER or HORNSEA, THE HESITANT RESORT.

Editors of local papers in the towns thus favoured were delighted to take us solemnly to task when occasion allowed (as, for instance, when we described Pudsey as 'the traditional home of the gormless'). We rarely ventured into politics but were occasionally dragged in, as on the occasion when Keighley Labour Party, under the headline LABOUR PARTY PROTEST TO MAGAZINE, published a letter in the *Keighley News* protesting against our 'failure' to contact the leader of the Labour group on the local council when gathering the material for our article. Writing from 'the wrong side of the railway tracks', as he put it, the writer alleged that whenever anyone took it upon himself to write about Keighley, he invariably 'went to the old establishment'.

He urged us to be more factual and less prone to 'a kind of faded cynicism'. It was a well-written and doubtless sincere letter, and I must admit I took a certain pride in my own reply now peeling from the same page of my cuttings book. 'It is easy,' I concluded ponderously, 'to write articles so full of facts as to be unreadable, and one might argue that cynicism, however faded, is preferable to the doctrinaire attitude which alienates many otherwise sympathetic people from your party.'

No doubt I was naïve, but being anything but a political animal, I have never been able to understand the determination of the politically inclined to divide the whole population into opposing teams when there can be no doubt that good men, as well as scoundrels, have found themselves at home in parties of every persuasion.

It also puzzled me that a so-called 'glossy' magazine (which I never considered *Yorkshire Life* to be, except in a strictly literal sense) should be automatically assumed to be Tory. The publishers, as I was to discover, almost certainly took it for granted that it could hardly be anything else. Rather belatedly I began to realise that unwittingly I had moved into a different world.

Until I joined the Navy and widened my horizons in every sense, I had assumed that no one with either brains or integrity would dream of voting anything but Labour. Still influenced by that kind of mental background, but without any intentional bias, I introduced a series of articles by Yorkshire Members of Parliament, blithely kicking off with a piece by the Hon. Member for Dewsbury (Labour, of course). He was probably as delighted to accede to my request as some of my directors were bemused in reading the results.

Perhaps because I was sincere in my wayward notions and insisted on what I saw as my editorial rights, I always came up (as someone wonderingly said) 'smelling of roses'. Whatever you write about, you stand a fair chance of infuriating someone. Even when you are trying your hardest to let the milk of human kindness flow from your pen, the results can be seen as positively vitriolic – and the glossier your pages and the more circumscribed your sphere, the greater is the risk. If you decide to play safe you might try writing about bluebells or long-dead local worthies, but even that is no guarantee of safety. I once had a phone call from a descendant of one of Yorkshire's many famous eccentrics, demanding to know who had taken it upon himself to write about her ancestor. She'd certainly like to meet him! She'd tell him a thing or two he didn't know. Yorkshire folk, it seemed, had a copyright on their forebears and eccentricity appeared to be genetically transmitted.

Once I poked gentle fun in the magazine at the pupils of some school who had produced an account of their area, full of youthful solecisms and reading almost as hilariously, I thought, as *1066 and All That*. I was astonished to receive a letter from the headmaster of the school roundly reproaching me for my insensitivity. His indignation was so genuinely inspired by pride in his pupils' achievement and his desire to defend them that I could only apologise and protest my innocence of any cruel intent. I am glad to say that he accepted my explanation in the most generous and friendly spirit.

It is so easy to yield to the impulse to take a rise out of somebody, but the results can be nothing short of disastrous. This truth is most quickly learned by writers who are in fairly close contact with their readers. The farther you are from your public, the greater is the tendency to see them as distant non-entities whose feelings can be safely ignored. If some writers on the national media could see at first hand the results of their ill-considered attempts at humour they might hesitate a little longer before playing the wag.

Yet even sensitivity can be overdone. At least, I thought so when one of my headlines on the old *Yorkshire Evening News* came in for criticism. The story I was handling concerned a schoolboy making his way home through a park containing a partially dried up lake. The lad's name was Dick and, boy-like, in order to shorten his journey home he decided to cross the dried-up lake, with results predictable by anyone but him: he got stuck in the mud, but was safely rescued (possibly with the help of the fire brigade) without having suffered any ill effects.

The *Evening News*, as a 'bright' newspaper, specialised in lively headlines of the kind I strove to write. The boy's name, I mused, was Dick; Dick had been stuck in the mud while trying to take a short cut, so what better headline could there be than NO SHORT CUT FOR DICK-IN-THE-MUD, which fitted perfectly into the headline style prescribed by the chief sub?

I tossed the copy across the table into his basket. He sent it to the type-setters after a glance only marginally briefer than my satisfaction proved to be when the paper appeared and an assistant editor, who long ago put his last edition to bed, berated me for my lack of feeling. How, he demanded, would I feel on seeing that headline had I been the lad's mother? Since all had ended happily, I felt I would have been relieved enough to join in the joke; but clearly it was a joke my superior quite failed to see.

I HAD gravitated to the *Yorkshire Evening News* from Huddersfield, after some five years in the delightful company of Bill Lowis and his crew, only to wonder why I'd done it. Life on the *Examiner* was pleasant and amusing. Perhaps it was the prospect of a few pounds a week more that swayed me, having recently become the father of my first child, Anne, but I soon wondered if I'd made a mistake.

The *Evening News* offices were in Trinity Street, Leeds, which took its name from the nearby Holy Trinity Church, one of the architectural sights of Leeds, a Georgian building locally known as 'the Wedding Cake' on account of its distinctive spire. And in Trinity Street the atmosphere was as unlike that of the *Examiner* as it could be. Instead of the rather retiring Elliot Dodds, we had as editor the resoundingly named Ralph Waldo Shawcross, who could make the bravest tremble as he scrutinised each edition as it came off the press. Suddenly, 'I say . . .' he would begin ominously. A pause, then, 'Who did so-and-so?' and none trembled more than he who had to say, 'I did'.

In RR's time on the *Batley News*, competition with our weekly contemporary had been keen in all conscience, but compared with the *Evening News* staff's war with the *Evening Post* it had been mere fun and games. Hence the following conversation in the subs' room of the *Yorkshire Evening News* after the chief sub, Alan Weir, had trustingly handed me the front page lead – a sea rescue story from the Yorkshire coast.

'There's a good story from Bridlington,' called Alan across the room to whichever executive was standing in for the editor just then. The response was less than enthusiastic: nevertheless, the story remained the 'lead' in the expectation that it might be changed for the next edition if something better turned up. Meanwhile, I did my best, as instructed, to contain the graphic details of the rescue beneath their banner headlines in a mere half-column of type.

For perhaps half an hour, what passed as peace reigned in the subs' room – then the first edition of the *Evening Post* arrived. Its front page struck horror in all who saw it. For our competing organ, too, had 'led' with the rescue, but against the modest half-column into which I had obediently crammed all the facts I could, 'they' had filled the whole front page with interviews and pictures. And the type they had used would have been big enough for the announcement of World War Three.

For the opposition to have outshone us in any way was seen as a disaster. As usual, the disaster was followed by an inquest.

'I told you it was a good story,' said Alan in his patient, resigned Scottish way to the executive whose instructions he had followed.

'You didn't tell me it was a hell of a story,' that worthy replied.

BACK to my cuttings books, wherein I find a photograph captioned: 'The Mayoress persuades author John Moore (right) to autograph a copy of his book *Portrait of Elmbury*' (as if any author ever needed such 'persuasion'). Along with these two luminaries, I can just recognise a youthful editor of *Yorkshire Life*, together with the then Mayor of Wakefield and various other dignitaries. The occasion was a dinner at Wakefield Town Hall to celebrate some such occasion as National Library Week: John Moore and I were two of the three speakers, the third being Moore's publisher.

I had accepted the invitation with trepidation, for I was no orator. Seated at the top table in a crowded banqueting hall, I ate little and made polite conversation even less. The fact that I had managed to persuade myself to attend such a function at all proves, if it proves anything, that my determination to promote *Yorkshire Life* on such a 'literary' occasion was even greater than my dread of standing before this large gathering and hearing my own voice raised in solo performance. For weeks I had agonised over my speech, which was supposed to occupy twenty minutes. What would they think of it? How would it stand up against the competition of two such weighty performers as John Moore and his doubtless erudite and witty publisher?

I was the third to speak and so had the doubtful privilege of listening to my forerunners through a kind of auditory fog, dismally conscious that they seemed to be going down very well. My own approaching share in the proceedings bore a striking resemblance to death in its terrible inevitability. When it arrived, I rose on uncertain legs and produced from my inside pocket the pages of typescript over which I had laboured so earnestly.

What sort of a talk would they expect, these presumably bookish people who had spent five guineas or so of hard-earned brass (this happened some thirty years ago) to listen to three speeches and eat one dinner in the elevated company of the civic heads of Wakefield?

Clearly my peroration had to have a bookish element, and, if possible a Wakefield theme. I had swotted up on George Gissing, the ill-starred, Wakefield-born novelist who died, aged forty-six in 1903 after a life of poverty and ill health. Probably no more than two or three of my audience had read the works of this distinguished son of what used to be called the 'Merry City'. They might have been surprised to learn that I had never read Gissing either. But at least I knew that every audience everywhere – with the possible exception of the congregation at a funeral – wants most of all to *laugh*.

'At Batley, where I live,' I began, 'a millowner decided to name his palatial mansion "The Cloisters" – because it was cloise ter t' mill, cloise ter t' pub and cloise ter t' station . . .' Perhaps it was sympathy, or it may have been relief that I and not they stood defenceless at the top table with a half-digested meal inside me. Perhaps they were simply glad that my speech was the last. But whatever the reason, a gale of genuine and surprised amusement rose from the tables and blew my nervousness away.

Encouraged, I proceeded to tell them how this same captain of industry had decided that a cultivated man, such as he aspired to be, ought to exhibit his culture by lining his rooms with books. He therefore summoned a bookseller to *The Cloisters*, escorted him to the vast library with its lofty walls, told him what was required and enquired 'how much a foot' he would charge to do the job. My 'bookish' audience loved it, my fellow speakers congratulated me and if George Gissing was there in spirit, I hope he forgave me for placing him in such ridiculous company as the man who lived at *The Cloisters*.

ONE of the strangest of my cuttings was culled in 1980 from the monthly journal of the Yorkshire Arts Association, which had included my name and business telephone number in a directory of Yorkshire writers. My office was at Otley then, but the Otley telephone code had been inadvertently omitted from the entry. Some readers tried to reach me by using the Leeds code – only to hear the sinister tones of a man claiming to be the 'Yorkshire Ripper', as he speculated on where his next 'strike' might be and taunted the police with their lack of success.

What they heard was a voice tape which had been made available by the police to the public via the Leeds number in the hope that this would help in the hunt for the killer. With the conviction of Peter Sutcliffe, the tape was proved to have been the mischievous work of a hoaxer, but the unexpected voice must have caused a shiver or two to some people who sought merely to contact a harmless editor.

At least the incident gave the magazine some piquant publicity. The local press were obviously amused that the episode should have involved what one paper called such a 'highly respectable' magazine, and an old friend of mine, the *Yorkshire Evening Post* columnist who wrote as John Wellington, rightly commended the candour of the Yorkshire Arts Association in immediately publishing a correction and apology.

19
How to be
a family man

A FAVOURITE phrase of my mother's when faced with humour that verged even slightly on the ridiculous, was '*too daft to laugh at*', uttered with a contemptuous pursing of the lips. This intrigued me mightily when I first heard it, for if some things were *too* daft to laugh at, there must be other things which were *just about* daft enough and others not daft enough to raise the faintest smile. In her scale of daftness, Charlie Chaplin probably held top place as the world's daftest comedian. Laurel and Hardy were probably daft enough to laugh at in the unlikely event that she'd nothing better to do.

My mother, I should explain, along with many other women of her day, laughed not so much when they were amused as when they were happy – which usually meant when their husbands and children were happy. Female laughter of that period, according to Colbeck's Theory, would seem to be a manifestation of relief from domestic stress rather than an expression of joy at the sheer crazy upside-downness of life. Working class women between the wars were not over-endowed with a sense of humour: they hadn't time for such frivolling so they left it to the men.

One thing my mother found it easy to laugh at was me – when she wasn't crying over me, that is. She even laughed at my jokes when she recognised them as such. It was probably this that gave me the notion that I was destined to be a sort of Yorkshire Mark Twain. Hence my first adult hardback, *How to be a Family Man.*

Like many a better book, it came into existence almost by accident. One day in 1965 there came into my office for review a book called *Hubert Calendar Counts His Blessings*. The author was one Patrick Ryan, a *Punch* contributor of such eminence that he was a member of the famous 'Table'. Patrick, I learned from the blurb, though born in the Old Kent Road, had improved on his humble origins to such a degree that he was now Head Postmaster at Harrogate no less!

Also from the blurb, I learned that he was the author of 'the riotous *How I Won the War*', which the *Yorkshire Evening Post* had called 'one of the funniest pieces of writing to come out of the Second World War'. A fact of great consequence at the time was that this book had been made into a film starring arch-Beatle John Lennon.

In those days I took humour very seriously, believing that even if it could hardly save the whale or the planet, it might possibly revive the circulation figures of *Yorkshire Life*, which had become rather static. So I took Patrick to lunch at Harrogate's Prospect Hotel and suggested he write a series of articles on the theme 'How I became a Yorkshireman'. It was agreed that he should write an initial six, after which we were to review the situation – and the fee.

From the very first article, the series was a winner. For a 'lah di dah southerner' (as his fictitious Yorkshire employer Mr Micklethwaite called him), Patrick showed an amazingly accurate grasp of life in his adopted county. His first lesson from the outrageous Mr Micklethwaite convinced him, for instance, that contempt was the only proper Yorkshire attitude to what his employer called 'a bloody umber-ella', clearly an article no self-respecting Yorkist would be found dead beneath.

Succeeding lessons covered such weighty matters as neighbourliness, the art of being 'owned by a Yorkshire Terrier', cricket and 't'League' (Rugby League, of course). The final article described the presentation of Patrick's accolade, won during his first year as an apprentice Tyke – a flat cap, adorned with a plastic white rose, and a square foot of genuine Yorkshire pudding.

Mr Micklethwaite may have been a composite caricature of every comic Yorkshireman who ever drew fictional breath, but the readers loved him. I can think of no other series which had shown anything like the circulation-building appeal of *How I Became a Yorkshireman*.

For the agreed six months the series ran its triumphant course, where-upon, by spontaneous mutual agreement, it was launched on a further voyage. Only after fifteen articles, when Patrick felt he had exhausted the possibilities and completed his fictional novitiate, did we agree to present him with his accolade as a fully qualified Tyke. Then, presumably exhausted by his arduous quest, he migrated to a new post at somewhere like Henley-on-Thames. I hope he enjoyed his stay here and had many a retrospective chuckle. If adding to the laughter of a supposedly dour county is any kind of an achievement he had certainly not wasted his time among us. Further-more he had a pleasant souvenir in the book in which Frederick Muller collected his *Yorkshire Life* pieces.

But how was I to replace what had become my most popular series?

Whom did I know who had Patrick's rib-tickling touch? Nobody! Yet it had been proved beyond doubt that a monthly dose of laughter was a sure prescription for improving the circulation. Thus began a series by my humble self recounting imaginary personal disasters under the general heading *This Only Happens to Me*. It didn't make the same immediate impact as Patrick's series, but perhaps it filled a gap. At least the sales of *Yorkshire Life* did not plummet with his departure.

In due course I sent a selection of these pieces to Frederick Muller, who invited me to call and see them, if and when convenient, at their offices in Fleet Street. Convenient? I'd make sure it was convenient! Thus, confident that I had at last arrived, I found myself lunching in a Fleet Street restaurant with one of Muller's editors, who told me that he liked my stuff because it was subtle, and explained how we might be of use to each other.

Muller, it seemed, was in the course of producing a series of humorous illustrated books on such themes as *How to Live with a Neurotic Dog* and *How to be a Motorist and Stay Happy*. The editor thought I might be able to produce something on similar lines and that the illustrator of the *Yorkshire Life* series, Bill Geldart, then head of our magazine group's art department, might supply the drawings.

I travelled home with a positive sense of euphoria. What, I wondered, would my fellow passengers on the train from King's Cross think if they had any idea that I was not, like them, simply rattling along the lines to another railway station, but *en route* to a brilliant future?

It wasn't to be quite that easy. To start with, Muller insisted that in order to fit in with the series, my stories must be written in the third person. 'I can't do that,' I said. 'I can only make fun of myself – in print, anyway.' But that was how the other books in the series were written, they told me.

Friends to whom I complained glibly told me I should tell the publisher where to get off. 'It's your book isn't it? Who are they to tell you how to write it?' Yet in spite of their advice and my own misgivings, I agreed to do it Muller's way – partly because I saw the commission as a challenge. First, though, I was required to write a specimen chapter that would convince the publisher I could deliver the goods.

Here, my first mistake was to stick too close to real life in plotting my supposedly fictional adventures. For instance, their reaction when I offered them 'The Day the Dane Came' almost reduced me to despair. They insisted that it was too far-fetched, although it was, in fact, barely more than the literal truth.

The Dane, let me explain, was a dog, a Great Dane, which had been found exhausted in a corner of my garage one bitter winter's night. I was first made aware of its presence when I found myself prevented from entering my garage by my wife, striking a somewhat heroic pose, arms outstretched at the entrance. She had found the great gangling hound there when she returned from shopping. Looking as miserable as only a Great Dane knows how, it lay on a few whisps of straw intended for the guinea pigs' beds.

I left the car outside the garage and inspected the new lodger as it lay shivering and exhausted. Somehow it managed to stagger with me into the house, pausing to reconnoitre the kitchen, where, with one lick of a two-foot long tongue, it took in the cat's dinner. From there it staggered into the living-room, whereupon the cat ran three times round the walls like a wall-of-death rider, before disappearing up the chimney. Or that was my impression at the time.

The dog was now lying in front of our fire, almost covering the entire floor, while its ribs heaved and its breath really did rattle in and out of its chest.

A call to the police station elicited the less than helpful fact that no dog answering to my description had been reported missing. Precisely how we accommodated said dog that night I do not remember: I can only say that it neither shared our bed, nor was it turned out into the garage. To the precise terms agreed between it and the cat I was not privy, nor would I swear that the dog ever actually noticed it: it was, after all, a small cat. The Dane, though far from small, was entirely amiable, responding with equanimity and good manners to whatever we proposed for its welfare. There were moments when it seemed we were stuck with it for life: but it showed no signs of homesickness.

Next morning a further call to the police revealed that a businessman with premises in Batley but living in Leeds had reported the dog missing. It had been absent when the time came for him to shut up shop and go home, and having made whatever efforts he considered appropriate to locate his wandering dog, home he went to the big city, possibly hoping that he would find the animal there when he arrived.

Man to dog, I explained the situation. 'We've enjoyed your company', I said, 'but the best of friends must part. If you'll just sidle into the car I'll take you to meet the nice policeman who'll look after you until your boss collects you'. Being a perfect gentledog he understood the situation immediately, lolloped on to the back seat of my car with perfect composure and was conveyed to the cop-shop. I never heard from his owner, so was unable to sue him for the price of fourteen tins of Kit-e-Kat – or maybe it was only thirteen.

One of the kinder provisions of nature seems to be an instinct, shared perhaps by both animals and humans, that enables them when in trouble to know exactly where to look for help. There was the big black rabbit which appeared on my front lawn one December evening, was given 'temporary' refuge to protect it from savage dogs, starvation or the bitter weather – and stayed eight years. And there was also, most remarkably, the Lady Who came from the Night . . .

It was, in fact, in the early hours of the morning that I heard a persistent knocking at our door. Reluctantly and with trepidation I answered it, to find her standing in some distress on my doorstep – wearing only one shoe (plus clothes, of course). I think she said she had been attacked by a man whose taxi she had shared. What precisely had happened to the attacker and the taxi-driver is no longer clear in my mind, but certainly they were no longer present.

This happened at the height of the 'Ripper' terror, when the police in the North of England were desperately seeking the perpetrator of a series of murders of women in the Leeds and Bradford area. I rang the police who in due course arrived at our house in the form of two women officers, who offered to take charge of our guest.

For reasons no longer clear, this led to an argument between police and guest, the latter, for whatever reason, being apparently quite happy to remain where she was. Eventually the situation was resolved. The guest departed rather reluctantly, assuring me she would write. I went to bed wondering how far into the night the Ripper, or another of his ilk, might have travelled by now on his murderous way.

Comic, or too daft (or tragic) to laugh at? My mother would have known.

20
Phyllis
and others

HUDDERSFIELD and Halifax are inextricably linked in my memory. Not only because they are a mere cock-stride apart, but because they are so closely related in their situation and history that they ought really to resemble each other. Each is an industrial town on the edge of the moors, each the 'capital' of a so-called metropolitan district – in the case of Huddersfield it is 'Kirklees' and in the case of Halifax 'Calderdale' – yet each to me presents a very different personality.

Who, I wonder in passing, chooses the names of newly created authorities? I would never suspect a bureaucrat of being a romantic, yet on what else but romantic grounds could the name Kirklees, with its Robin Hood associations, have been chosen for a local government area that can include places as disparate as Holmfirth and Heckmondwike.

And what about Calderdale as title for the metropolitan district which has Halifax as its centre? Had she lived long enough, I might have asked Phyllis Bentley, the grande dame of literary Halifax, for her opinion about that. She would have seen it as her civic duty to oblige me, even though Phyllis and I did not always see eye to eye.

When I first became editor of *Yorkshire Life* I regarded Yorkshire's doyenne of regional writers with something of the dutiful awe felt by her coterie of admirers in the Halifax Authors' Circle or the much-loved Civic Theatre. For she was one of the Yorkshire novelists it was my solemn intention to foster, promote and cultivate. They were entitled, I felt, to a deal more honour in their own county than they were getting.

In retrospect I think some of them may have been getting more than their share. Yorkshire folk, generally speaking, are not social climbers in the accepted sense; they rarely suck up to their betters for the very good reason that they are sure they have none, but when it comes to idolatry of those whose accomplishments they admire they can be positively sycophantic.

Characteristically, though, their admiration is anything but blind. They know perfectly well that their idols are less than perfect; they admit it freely, and forgive them.

Phyllis on one occasion was less than forgiving to me, but it was partly my own rather ridiculous fault for having fallen victim to an attack of neuralgia on the day I interviewed her. Things started going wrong from there. It was the sort of sadistic affliction which leaves you alone just long enough to make you think it will never come back, and then descends on you with a fury all the greater for having left you blissfully in peace for half an hour. I knew I had arrived unconscionably early for my date with the author of *Inheritance, et al*, that day in Halifax, but my neuralgia had miraculously abated and I knew that if I delayed my visit I might be incapacitated for the rest of that day.

From the moment she opened the door, I knew that I had miscalculated. I could hardly have quoted neuralgia as my reason for arriving early. I might, of course, have assured her that my intense impatience to meet her would brook no delay, but Phyllis would never have fallen for that. Perhaps I didn't know enough then about women – including women novelists – to realise that the unforgivable offence is to arrive earlier than you have promised, thus denying them sufficient time to prepare, emotionally and otherwise, for the ordeal in store.

She had been nothing less than enthusiastic in her reply to my letter requesting an audience. She had enjoyed, she said, reading my interview with Sooty, the late Harry Corbett's televisual accomplice, but this encouraging start only made the failure of the actual event the more disappointing. True, she answered my foolish questions politely and submitted patiently to the requirements of my photographer, but I knew that somehow we had not 'hit it off' and the knowledge did nothing to help me produce a memorable piece.

When, as agreed, I let her see a copy of my article, she wrote a number of unflattering comments on it and said I had made her appear 'overbearing'. ('Well, of course, she *is*,' said a close friend of both of us when I told him.) It probably didn't help when, in my reply to her letter, I innocently protested that I had simply tried to present her as she was! (I don't think I actually said 'warts and all'.) Anyway, I felt I couldn't, in the event, use the piece since it offended her so much. She greeted my decision with a one-line letter: 'Thank you!'

Eventually I used the photographs taken during the interview (all, that is, except one which she said made her look 'like an invalid on a *chaise longue*') to illustrate a profile of her written by her old friends Marie Hartley and Joan Ingilby. There were other occasions when I unintentionally displeased Phyllis, and she did not hesitate to tell me so. She was a sensitive, proud and possibly lonely woman, who mellowed sufficiently with age to tolerate me a little better than she did on our ill-starred first encounter.

My dear old friend Cyril Lindley, who, if heaven needs a patron saint of photographers, should be seriously considered for the post, could usually restore good relations which, somehow or other, I had unwittingly disrupted – especially with women. Having met him once, Lady Cecilia Howard, then the chatelaine of Castle Howard, referred to him with a kind of rapture as 'that heavenly man', and there were doubtless many who would echo the description.

'Who is that *nice* man?' I was once asked by another interviewee, an actress of some fame, while Cyril was briefly absent from the scene: she clearly didn't mean me. Such misgivings would never have troubled Cyril. His attitude was rarely less than angelic – except to bossy bores who took him by the sleeve and told him what to photograph. Then he would dig in his heels with an almost audible crunch.

Cyril had a gentleness not always found in press photographers plus a determination to produce the pictures required of him at no matter what cost in time or effort. Once, alas, his dedication ran away with him, and again it was my fault. I can still go hot with shame when I remember how, with the most harmless intentions, I subjected Cyril to the wrath of J. B. Priestley, star speaker at a literary luncheon held by the *Yorkshire Post* in a Leeds hotel. I had it all worked out just how the two of us could produce an excellent feature from the event for *Yorkshire Life*.

'What we want,' I said, 'is a series of close-ups of J. B. making his speech – gestures, expressions, that sort of thing. We'll take these right across the centre spread and I'll use quotes from his talk as captions.'

Planted barely a dozen feet from the great man as he spoke from the top table, Cyril squinted into his view-finder and waited for J. B. to come up with the goods. And as Priestley rose to his pinnacles of eloquence, Cyril conscientiously and relentlessly clicked his camera – again – and again.

Although, years ago, I experienced an earth tremor in Naples, I have never waited at the foot of Vesuvius in the certainty that an eruption was imminent. But at least I know now how that might feel. Standing in the middle of the dining room, Cyril was beyond my reach. I could have thrown bits of bread at him, but I should only have missed; I could have left my seat and led him, protesting, from his post, where he stood like the Roman sentry in the painting *Faithful Unto Death*, or feigned a heart attack, but that would, if possible, have made matters worse. So I could only wait for Vesuvius, disguised as a portly Yorkshire author, to erupt.

As the *Yorkshire Post* mercilessly reported next day, 'a photographer' cut off the distinguished speaker 'in mid-sentence', with consequences, they might have added, that may have enlivened the event for those who had bought tickets, but added nothing to my own enjoyment.

'Haven't you got enough now?' growled Priestley, fixing poor Cyril with a baleful eye across the packed dining room at the Hotel Metropole or the Queen's, or wherever. 'This isn't easy, you know!' Overwhelmed by embarrassment, poor Cyril could only impersonate a beetroot and retreat from his vantage point, while J.B. neatly knotted the ends of his severed sentence and continued with his discourse. I remember at least one sentence from it: 'Cherish your rebels!' He said not another word about photographers. Not, at least, in public.

When the indefatigable Cyril, a gentleman even in his anguish, bravely sought out the celebrity to apologise and attempt an explanation, all he got was a grumbled 'Don't do it again!' I, meanwhile, less brave or less gentlemanly, was left with only my guilt, since Cyril after all had been merely fulfilling my wishes and doing it all too well. Undoubtedly a kindly man, Priestley was possibly feeling annoyed with himself for his outburst.

A minor incident this might seem in retrospect, but it was embarrassing at the time, not least because I had reason to be grateful to Priestley, for giving me quite a scoop in my earliest days with *Yorkshire Life*. I had planned a super Bradford issue, the main feature in which was to be written by my humble self. I was discussing this with a colleague, the seasoned Lancashire journalist George Eglin, formerly northern editor of Tom Hopkinson's great *Picture Post* and more recently editor of *Lancashire Life*, when someone mentioned Priestley.

'Why not ask him to write something?' suggested George. So in an unashamed begging letter, I explained to Priestley that I could not, alas, pay him the celebrity rates he merited, but the undersigned struggling editor would be extremely grateful, and so on. Oh, and by the way, if he had a suitable photograph of himself, we'd be grateful for that too.

Almost by return of post came what we used to call a quarto envelope bearing an Isle of Wight postmark. Could the great man really have replied so promptly? If my fingers had ever trembled opening a package, they did so as they extracted a typescript attached to a letter with a sprawling signature which unmistakably read 'J.B. Priestley'.

As I read it I could almost hear the rumbling, grumbling, tones of Priestley as he seemed to be going out of his way to disguise any appearance of graciousness. 'Your letter reached me when I'd a couple of hours with nothing to do,' he began. 'Since you can't afford to pay me my accustomed rates, don't pay me anything. Instead, when you get books to review with photographs of the Yorkshire Dales, please send them to me when you've done with them.' On one occasion when I sent him a rather borderline volume for good measure, he courteously returned it. Not that he would have been a loser if I had never sent him one, because the publicity he (and of course the magazine) subsequently received in the Yorkshire press would have cost hundreds, if not thousands, even then, in advertising terms.

During the possibly mythical two hours 'with nothing to do' mentioned in his letter, he had composed what he modestly entitled a 'Note by a Young Bradfordian' in which he compared the Bradford of his boyhood with the Bradford of 1956 – and not, need I add, to the latter's advantage.

And so, in the October 1956 issue of *Yorkshire Life*, the second issue I had edited, alongside the Douglas Glass portrait photograph he had suggested, Priestley firmly put the city that bore him in its place. In the Olympian tones of a man who had travelled far beyond the boundaries of the wool metropolis, he declared that Bradford was no longer the Bradford he had known and loved. It was becoming increasingly indistinguishable from 'a town in the American mid-west'. Indeed, he declared, it had only to lose a few more of the treasures that had been its glory in his boyhood – another theatre, concert hall or arcade – to be identical with a town in the mid-west.

It was clear that he wished to be understood as speaking more in sorrow that in anger; and that, although in his view the Bradford of 1956 was not a patch on that of 1916, it was still no mean city. And furthermore that while he, as a Bradford lad born and bred, was privileged to knock it, lesser men from Leeds or London had better keep their mouths tight shut.

Perhaps the men from Leeds and London did just that, but Priestley's fellow citizens did no such thing. Having read copious extracts from Priestley's 'Note' in the *Yorkshire Post*, the *Evening Post*, the *Yorkshire Observer* and doubtless other organs to which I had sent complimentary copies, they leapt to fill the correspondence columns with their forthright opinions of Priestley and his uninvited and unwelcome views. As far as they were concerned, if Priestley could find nowt good to say about Bradford, he'd better stop in t' Isle of Wight or wherever the bloody hell he was living.

And doubtless, as he savoured their indignation, Priestley chuckled. He knew as well as anyone that Yorkshire celebrities are seen by fellow Tykes rather as pieces of public property who owe their success entirely to their county and its people for having allowed them the privilege of being born within its boundaries. The county's great, one feels, are viewed rather as gifted pets, who should be properly grateful that you have watched them perform on the field of sport, endured their euphonium solos or even, in extreme cases, borrowed their books from the public library.

Their success, it seems, however glorious, is due less to their own efforts than to the forbearance of the rest of us in allowing them to distinguish themselves so immodestly from the common herd. A similar view was taken of Fiery Fred Trueman when he passed some choice remarks about the Yorkshire cricket selectors. Heads were shaken and Yorkshiremen agonised over whether or not they'd allowed the lad to get above himself.

My mother-in-law took a similarly proprietorial view of the Royal Family, especially of its older and/or younger members, who invariably in her view wore the wrong clothes or facial expressions or otherwise exhibited an inappropriate public image, causing her to complain with as much heartfelt indignation as she would of her own grandchildren when she thought it necessary. In the case of the latter, of course, she would have laid an absolute claim to the privilage, while vigorously denying any such rights to others.

But royalty is royalty, even in Yorkshire. Unlike some other nations we have allowed our monarchs, or most of them to retain their heads and provided they did a good job, we have treated them with a reasonable amount of respect. Genius is different – it has always been troubled by fleas. A female of that species, who knew how to spell a word, once asked Dr Johnson how he could have got it wrong in his dictionary. His reply, 'Ignorance, ma'am, pure ignorance,' bore the stamp of a truly Christian tolerance. As a Yorkshireman, Priestley was cast in a different mould. Legend tells that when a gushing admirer told him *The Good Companions* was the greatest book he had ever written, he merely growled, 'So what's wrong with *Angel Pavement*?'

21
Learning
from 'Life'

I STARTED my career as editor of *Yorkshire Life* under the naïve misapprehension that everyone in Yorkshire shared my view of life and society. Some were richer, some poorer, of course; some voted Labour and some, incomprehensibly, I thought, Conservative; some were Catholic and some Protestant. But these differences apart – and they were superficial in my eyes – all Yorkshire folk were the same at heart. It was with a degree almost of unbelief that I gradually discovered how wrong I was.

In my corner of the world we never besought God to 'bless the squire and his relations and keep us in our proper stations'. We were brought up in the knowledge – it was more than a mere belief – that in terms of human value we were as good as the King himself, let alone the squire, whoever he might be. Certainly I wanted a life different from that my parents had known, but not because I saw their 'station' as in any way inferior. I admired their courage and cheerfulness, but I wanted freedom from the boredom of repetitive, unfulfilling toil they seemed to tolerate so stoically. Yet was it so surprising that after four years as a private in the First World War, my father must have been more than merely tolerant of the trifling hardships of civvy street?

These being my beliefs, I had never considered the word 'county' as more than a geographical term. In my view, a 'county magazine' was simply, by definition, a magazine for readers interested in a particular county. The idea of 'the County' as a kind of patrician super class struck me as ludicrous if not obnoxious. So I never accepted the term as a label for the kind of magazine I was trying to produce. Instead I would describe it as 'regional'; for that, undoubtedly, it was. As for the term 'provincial', which clearly implied inferiority *vis-à-vis* the capital, my Yorkshire blood boiled up in rejection of that! Perhaps we've inherited more from the

Vikings whose kings once ruled from York than a dialect laced with Scandinavian words.

Considering my views (which I don't think they suspected for a moment any more than I understood theirs), I must have been something of a trial to my employers. Kindly, civilised men, they were apparently disposed to like me and full of praise for my early efforts as editor. Initially, luck was on my side: for one thing, I was fortunate to be the first full-time editor *Yorkshire Life* had known. Until my arrival, the editors of *Cheshire Life* (Leslie N. Radcliffe) and *Lancashire Life* (George Eglin) with whom I worked in the hardly salubrious purlieus of Phillips Park, Manchester, had made time to edit *Yorkshire Life* when their own magazines had been put to bed.

'Mr Bernard', however, Bernard Nicholls, company chairman and son of the founder of the printing company which then owned the group, had some doubts about my editorial policy, and these he confided to Leslie Radcliffe, our amiable and long-suffering editor-in-chief.

Leslie, in turn, would confide them to me. 'The chairman thinks you're in danger of becoming a bit too cloth cap, dear boy.' What could I say? The chairman's values and mine were completely at odds. I saw the magazine as a vehicle for news and comment on Yorkshire's people, rich or poor, high or low – it didn't matter as long as they were interesting and had something to say or were doing something worth writing about. The chairman, as a hunting man, said Leslie, wondered why I never published features about Yorkshire's hunts. of which there were apparently a great many – far too many, I would have said, my sympathies on the whole being with the hunted.

Since then my views have moderated. I prefer nature in symbiotic, rather than predatory mood, but the latter seems to predominate and we must come to terms with it as best we can. Meanwhile, I had to come to terms with the chairman and his views. Somehow or other, I never considered the possibility that he might solve the problem by dispensing with my services, though perhaps *he* did.

In the October issue of the magazine, in the recently acquired knowledge that the next month would see the start of the fox hunting season, I published an article under my own name entitled 'Fox-hunting – a Sport for Sentimentalists' and on the same 'spread' a 'reply' by the doyen of Yorkshire sporting writers and my oldest contributor (whose name and title, incidentally, took up more space than any other), Major J. Fairfax-Blakeborough.

From the moment I first met him we had been friends despite the enormous differences between us. I had inherited him when I first took the job and perhaps he viewed me kindly for keeping him on my contributors' payroll. Anyway, somehow or other we hit it off from our first meeting, on Catterick racecourse, where he was clerk of the course. When I asked him what he thought of the *Yorkshire Life* I was turning out, he answered, 'I think you've brightened it up no end, m'dear chap'.

We could hardly fail to be friends after that, so, reluctantly or not, JFB agreed to write the 'for' article in my fox-hunting debate. Looking at it now, I wonder how I got away with it. Titled in bold italic type reminiscent (in the chairman's eyes at least) of tabloid sensationalism and illustrated with a photograph provided by the League Against Cruel Sports, it was calculated, some thought, to bring 'Mr Bernard' to the point of apoplexy. Happily, its only result was a trickle of letters from writers on both sides of the hunting fence, and certainly not enough to indicate any considerable weight of opinion either way.

In solemn conclave with Leslie, 'Mr Bernard' had apparently expressed a wish (perhaps it was more than that) that the magazine should devote more space to county 'personalities' and had helpfully contributed some names of his own. I was less than tolerant of these invasions of my editorial autonomy and since I never hesitated to say so, soon gained a reputation for being disputatious: 'You'd argue about the length of a midge's didge,' sighed Harry Brewood, then managing director, with whom I had an almost classic love-hate relationship. My fury when, during his time as group advertisement manager, he removed the crossword puzzle from an issue in preparation without seeking my agreement became almost a matter of legend.

Harry would bet on anything – even the most ridiculous propositions. A wartime physical training instructor, he was proud of his strength and fitness, which he frequently offered to demonstrate. On one occasion he challenged me to a race, running backwards, up Prince Street in Bradford, where my office then was. No doubt he would have beaten me – at six foot something, as against my five foot six, he had a considerable advantage in leg-length, but even without that, he would inevitably have won, simply by putting his entire heart and soul into the ludicrous exercise, something I could never have brought myself to do.

There were occasions, however, when even I could beat Harry at his own game of one-upmanship. We were speculating one day on what the magazine's six-monthly circulation figures would reveal. Inevitably our forecasts differed. What they exactly were I can't recall. I only know that my figure exceeded his and instinctively, of course, he saw this as a challenge. To Harry, challenges were there to be accepted. So, at his suggestion we each placed a pound note (this was the sixties, remember) in an envelope and solemnly handed this to my secretary with instructions that under no circumstances must the envelope be opened before the half-yearly 'ABC' (Audit Bureau of Circulations) figures had been declared. Then it would be winner take all.

The day of revelation dawned at last. A memo arrived in Bradford from our Manchester head office with news of the figures. The envelope was opened and the truth revealed – we were 'up' – I'd won! I have known few moments of greater pleasure. There was no word acknowledging my victory in Harry's memo, but I wasn't going to let such a triumph slip by unremarked. Having first pocketed (if not spent) my winnings I told Harry of my victory.

'Ah yes,' he said, 'but you didn't tell me about the Delius Festival in Bradford, did you?'

The utter unexpectedness of this left me speechless. Otherwise I could have told him that when we had made the bet, I had known no more than he did that in 1962 Bradford would honour its son Frederick Delius on the centenary of his birth, with dinners, concerts and other civic junketings, and that by featuring these on a comparatively lavish scale in the magazine we should boost our circulation considerably in the six months concerned. By the time I was ready to reply, he had either disappeared or embarked on another topic much too weighty to interrupt with such trivia as our wager.

I was in fact the winner in a much deeper sense, because through the Delius Festival, not only did I acquire an undying love of Delius's music, but I had the privilege of meeting Eric Fenby, the one-time Scarborough organist who devoted so much of his youth to the last years of the querulous, paralysed genius who brought him to the verge of a breakdown.

Before meeting Fenby I had read his book, *Delius as I Knew Him*, which Sir Thomas Beecham, the greatest authority on the Bradford-born composer, described as 'a poignant and sometimes painful narrative by a highly sensitive youth of the last few years of an elderly man, blind and paralysed'.

There was, of course, much more to be said about Delius than that he was blind and paralysed. The paralysis was caused by syphilis, not a disease with which the young church organist Fenby was likely to be much acquainted. But Delius, while certainly elderly, was also a genius and it was this, together with Fenby's tragic devotion, that created a strange bond between them. That bond not only reunited the two at Delius's deathbed for the last five minutes of his life, but linked them strangely up to and even beyond the grave. For while Delius lay lifeless, Fenby, like a dutiful son, assisted the photographer who took a picture of the corpse, and the *mouler* who made a death mask and took an impression of the composer's right hand.

And it was again Fenby who, after the temporary burial of Delius at Grez sur Loing, accompanied the exhumed coffin of the unbelieving composer to England, where, with no word of commital, as Delius had instructed, it was buried in the country churchyard at Limpsfield, Surrey. I have often pictured the deeply religious Fenby standing at midnight beside Delius's lonely grave.

Even when the earth had covered the coffin, the bond was not broken, for when Bradford was the scene of that national festival honouring the centenary of the composer's birth, Fenby was a living link with Delius at the concert – an affair of dinner jackets, evening gowns and champagne – at Bradford's baroque Cartwright Memorial Hall.

A photograph in an old copy of *Yorkshire Life* brings it all to life again. From James Gunn's portrait on the stage, Delius turns sightless eyes on the city's notables. A few feet away Fenby, at Delius's old piano, accompanies the violinist Ralph Holmes, as he plays music which seems so exotic a fruit to have sprung from Bradford soil. Later, Fenby spoke to me in awed tones about a wonderful young cellist, Jacqueline du Pre (who sadly, never became old), playing Delius's *Sonata for cello and piano*. The soprano Heather Harper, accompanied by the legendary Ernest Lush, bewitched even the most down-to-earth of Bradford hearts with the unearthly beauty of Delius's songs.

What would Frederick himself have thought about it all? Bradford-born, as surely as John Boynton Priestley and from the same wool-nourished background, he had a harder road to travel than his fellow Freeman of the woollen city.

Some time before that concert I had interviewed Fenby at his Scarborough home in a room filled with Delius relics. Here were not only his grand piano, but the old gramophone with its huge horn, on which the maestro played the negro spirituals that reminded him of his days on the orange plantation in Florida, to which he had been reluctantly sent by his Prussian father, Julius, when it became apparent at last that his value to the family business of wool merchants was rather less than nil. After adventures amorous and otherwise (including a post as a cantor in a synagogue, because his looks allowed him to pass as Jewish), Delius eventually made his home at Grez sur Loing and it was here that illness finally made his life hardly bearable, inflicting its cruellest blow by rendering him incapable of composing.

Fenby told me how, as the young organist at Holy Trinity Church in Scarborough, he first came upon Delius's *Mass of Life* in a music shop and its beauty, as he put it, 'struck me to the heart'. From that moment he seemed unable to dismiss from his mind the stricken composer who, blind and paralysed, was unable to finish his life's work. Something must be done, Fenby felt, but who was to do it. He answered the irresistible call one night when sleep would not come until he had writen to Grez sur Loing offering what help he could. Fenby's heart must have sung with joy when he received a welcoming response with its invitation to visit Grez.

His meeting with Delius was far from encouraging. The stricken composer, gaunt and pale, could hardly summon enough strength to shake hands. Eric hesitated; Jelka, Delius's wife, gave him a glance of reassurance. He took the long, tapering fingers in his hand.

For some time nothing was said about the purpose of his visit. Then one day Delius sent for him and said he wanted to dictate a tune.

'Ter-ter-ter-ter-ter,' sang Delius. Fenby's heart sank. He asked the master to repeat the line. Delius did so on another note. What key was intended, asked the would-be amanuensis. Delius answered using German nomenclature, which left Fenby even more confused.

By then Delius was almost beside himself. 'I just couldn't go on any longer,' Eric told me. The sight of the great genius in his humiliation, struggling to express himself before 'a completely unknown musician' was more than he could bear. He excused himself and left the room. And as he went, he heard Delius say, 'That boy is useless'. It was probably only Jelka's entreaties that prevented Fenby leaving Grez that very night; and the discovery that men of the stature of Roger Quilter and Percy Grainger had already attempted the task and failed.

The next day Delius was in a kindlier mood. He asked Fenby to fetch one of his compositions, *A Poem of Life and Love*, and tell him what he thought of it. As he read the score, Fenby must have become even more convinced that he was attempting the impossible. This piece, he felt, read like something that might have been produced by an indifferent student of Delius.

What should he do, he enquired of Jelka. If he told Delius what he really thought, he would be off home on the next train! As on many future occasions, Jelka's wisdom saw him through. 'Tell him what you truly think,' she urged.

No doubt with the utmost misgiving, Fenby did so. Delius almost fell out of his chair with annoyance. Then, suddenly, he calmed down. 'Take it, my boy,' he said. 'Select all the good material and make a piece out of it yourself.' Eric did as he was bid, then, doubtless with mingled excitement and trepidation, waited for Delius to ask him to play it.

'Fenby,' said Delius when he had finished, 'you are an artist. You have set my mind in action after all this time.' Thus began the task which Beecham said was made possible only by Delius's iron resolution and Fenby's angelic patience.

22
The people
for to see

DEAR old Hermon Hall, the teacher who never raised his hand in anger, and rarely even his voice, probably said more things that I remember than any other of my teachers. Some I remember chiefly for losing their tempers, hurling chalk or sending me in disgrace for punishment by the headmaster. No doubt it was mostly my fault: they had a thankless task striving fruitlessly to introduce the rules of science or the principles of mathematics into my peculiarly resistant skull. They did their best (or worst) but it was Hermon, telling us, for instance, that your Englishman was 'never at home unless he was abroad', whose utterances have best weathered the unforgiving decades.

By those few casual words he probably gave me not only an early conception of travel as a fit and proper occupation for any Englishman worth his deerstalker and shooting stick, but also a fascination with paradoxical and quirky utterances. By misquoting book titles, so that *Behind Turkish Lattices* became *Behind Turkish Lettuces*, Hermon also conveyed the invaluable notion that language was something to play with. His lessons, if such they could be called, were liberally spiced with quotation and anecdote, often about the great and famous, but not infrequently about our parents whom he had taught. Could anybody really be that old? Only now, when I am even older than he was then, do I realise how much he influenced me.

Whether, in fact, Hermon had himself ever travelled, except in his imagination, I shall never know. Surprising as it seems to me now, he never quoted Keats's doggerel about the naughty boy who 'went away to Scotland, the people for to see' – or I'd remember it. But if he had, I should probably have wondered why such a natural and obvious state of affairs should have been considered worth writing about. After all. what better reason could there be for going anywhere than to see the people, and all the other things that we see at home but find different when we see them abroad, perhaps because that is the only time we really see them? Is this what Blake or somebody meant by 'the innocent eye' and what the blasé call naivety? If so, long may I be naïve.

I never entertained the notion that the Scots, for all their haggis eating and bagpipe blowing, were madly different from us in Yorkshire; yet when I first went to Scotland, just as when I first went to Africa or Russia, Israel, Thailand or Uzbekistan, it was with a kind of eager expectation that the very air I breathed would taste differently, and the knowledge that if it didn't I would be greatly disappointed.

In fact it always did. Even crossing the border into Lancashire to go to Blackpool was as much a voyage of discovery as those embarked upon by pith-helmeted heroes on the screens of the Plaza, the Regent, the Vic or that poshest of Batley's picture palaces, the Empire Super Cinema. And on the day we took a trip to Rhyl, I was overwhelmingly conscious that now at last I was in another country. If you'd asked when I was ten what I'd best like to be, I'd have told you, 'An explorer!'

The boy I talked with on the beach at Rhyl did not disappoint me, even though he was white all over, wore ordinary swimming trunks, carried no spear like the Masai warriors I had yet to meet, spoke English but entranced me by the Welshness of his accent. I was an embryo Englishman abroad and what I felt, with all due respect to Hermon Hall, was a great deal better than merely feeling 'at home'. Perhaps those lithographs of Stanley and Livingstone on the wall of my Albert Street home have a lot to answer for.

WHEN I went to the former USSR my desire 'the people for to see' was almost at fever pitch. I had visited Jugoslavia and Hungary, when they, too, were Communist, but actually to see the Communist people of the great Russian empire that seemed destined to last for ever, the country of Lenin and Stalin, of Chaliapin, Tolstoy and Chekhov . . . was it possible that even here I should find, like Keats's naughty boy, that the ground was as hard, that a yard was as long, that a song was as merry as in England? Never, never could it be.

And it wasn't. On the contrary. From the moment the plane began to descend in preparation for landing at Moscow, I felt an inward singing delight that everything was so unbelievably Russian – from the December snow out of which the dark green fir trees were rising, to the vast and apparently seatless arrival hall at the airport and the even vaster length of time we had to stand and wait there while two young, bored and incredibly slow-moving officials processed our entry to the realm of Ivan the Terrible, his heirs and successors.

Old Hermon Hall was right. I, at least, was one Englishman who was indeed peculiarly and joyfully 'at home' when abroad. Even the boredom of standing in a queue was touched with excitement because I was sharing in the boredom of the great Russian people. Surely my extravagant obsession with treading the alien corn leaves your average Anglophile or Francophile standing – I am what I can only call a xenophile! And if that strikes you as a mad thing to be, allow me to say that I'd rather be that than a xenophobe.

Much of my early post-war travelling was done at someone else's expense, in the hope that I might write about it and presumably help out the host country's economy by attracting tourists to the place. Thus I have visited Greece, Israel, France, Germany and Norway, to name but a few, filling in the remaining gaps when I could afford it by going at my own expense. Israel I have twice visited by invitation – once before and once after the 1967 war. I love the people, but find them sometimes infuriating, which is a pity, because they have suffered so much and are so touchingly anxious that you should enjoy the Promised Land. But one country at a time . . .

WE were in Leningrad. At least, that was what they called it then. Looking at its majestic broad streets and squares I felt nostalgic for its old name, St Petersburg, and never suspected, of course, that in a few short years it would bear that resounding name again. Across the hotel breakfast table sat our two female guides – one who was attached to our party for the whole of the tour, a beautiful, rather languid creature whom I shall call Sonya, and her formidable regional equivalent – the sort who met us at each halt along the way and remained with us until we moved on, by means of almost daily flights by Aeroflot. This latter lady I shall name Natasha.

Sonia it was who bore the burden of our undisciplined western ways throughout the whole trip, and got to know us well enough to ask, somewhat wistfully, if we lived in a house and had a garden. Like most of her equally curious compatriots, she seemed to treat our answers with polite incredulity. When two of our party had been long overdue returning to the coach after a visit to Moscow University – something between the Empire State Building and Westminster Abbey – it was Sonia who stood, sad-eyed as a Chekhov heroine, at the entrance to our coach, with snowflakes falling gently on her hair, grieving silently over their absence. The rest of us, being British, knew that there was 'always one' to be waited for, so bore the delay with stoic good humour. But we of course were not answerable to some power-hungry Soviet bureaucrat, who for all we knew had the power to send us to Siberia.

As the brief December dusk turned to darkness, the errant two reappeared, cheerfully impenitent as such always are, and scrambled aboard, smiling as complacently as if our reproaches were compliments.

'Thank God,' murmured Sonya.

'You're a Russian Communist,' I taunted her playfully. 'Communists don't thank God.'

'Oh yes they do', she sighed, with enormous relief.

BUT back to Leningrad and breakfast, which, I seem to remember, consisted principally of a meat ball drowning pathetically in a basin of pale, warm soup. Immediately across the table sat Sonya and Natasha, conversing, a little impolitely I felt, in Russian. Natasha, maybe sensing my disapproval, made an effort at social chit-chat. Where in Britain did we come from, she enquired, and what did I do? From Yorkshire, I said, and I was an editor.

Instantly Natasha forgot all about polite English conversation as she earnestly engaged Sonya in the language of Stalin and Rasputin. There could be no doubt that they were talking about me. Clearly the disclosure of my calling made me an object of greater interest than, for instance, a chartered accountant might have been. Precisely why that was so would be revealed in due course. Meanwhile our itinerary required us to visit the Hermitage where, incidentally, we met the Pioneers.

Any worthwhile tour of Russia would have to include the Hermitage, which hardly needs describing as one of the world's richest treasuries of art. On the day of our visit, the hundreds, probably thousands of other visitors included a lively party of youngsters, aged ten or eleven and distinguished by the red scarves which clearly served as a sort of uniform. Apart from that they were like any other group of kids of a similar age, with the inevitable show-off spurred on to excel himself by the excitement of an outing.

Natasha surveyed them fondly. They were Pioneers, she said (apparently members of a kind of State-run Boy Scout movement). When they reached the appointed age, it seemed, each Soviet child donned the red scarf which entitled him or her to embark on all kinds of beneficial activities, doubtless with the intention of becoming a good Communist. Clearly, in Natasha's eyes at least, this was a good thing. 'Every child in Russia is *bursting* to become a Pioneer.'

'*All* of them?'

'Oh, yes,' Natasha assured me, seeing this as further evidence of admirable Soviet egalitarianism.

'What if,' I said, 'they don't want to?' Natasha looked at me as if I were slightly unhinged. My wife gave me her can't-take-you-anywhere look. Then Natasha smiled a forgiving, uncomprehending smile. 'But they *do*,' she said. 'They *always* want to join.'

'But what happens if sometimes they don't?'

Natasha's smile became a trifle strained. The rest of the group began to find objects of fascinating interest all around the cavernous room.

'Well,' said Natasha, making a mental note to avoid any other party containing a Yorkshireman, 'nobody would be forced to join of course . . . but they do all want to . . . Now, if you will all please come this way, there is something of particular interest . . .'

Next day I awoke from a post-luncheon snooze to find Sonya smiling down at me, a pleasant enough way to wake up, though why she should have singled me out for her attentions I had no idea.

Did I know, she enquired, about Andropov walking out of the Geneva peace talks? Yes, of course. The Soviet leader's gesture had been big news a few days before we left England. But what, I wondered, had it to do with me? Her next words made me wake up rather quickly, because what it had to do with me was apparently an interview on the region's television service to ascertain my reactions to the collapse of the talks.

I must admit the idea had its attraction. 'What did you do when you were in Russia?' I would be asked on my return to Yorkshire. 'Oh, nothing much,' I might reply airily. 'It was a bit of a drag really. They would insist that I appeared on the box. Really, you can't go anywhere incognito these days . . .'

Our tour courier, a nice lass from Liverpool, did a very good impression of a mother hen having kittens. I mustn't even consider it, she said, and I had to admit that she was right. Fun though it sounded, this would be rather different from being interviewed on Yorkshire Telly in defence of the idea that Prince Andrew, as Duke of York, simply must be married in York Minster. This, in the old cold war days, or barely out of them, would clearly be a propaganda exercise during which I would have no idea how my remarks and answers were being presented to the viewer. I did know, though, that somehow or other I would be used to bolster the Soviet side, possibly to the detriment of ours.

And yet . . . somehow I couldn't help feeling that the mere fact that I am anything but a political animal might just possibly have got under their guard. One of my few regrets in life (though a very minor one) is that, for what seemed good and sound reasons, I was unable to do it. Still, I couldn't please both Sonya and the lass from Liverpool. Perhaps, all things considered, it was best that the lass from Liverpool won.

CEYLON – Sri Lanka as we call it now – was long regarded by some as the original Garden of Eden. But while that island, as I discovered during my two-year sojourn there, has many paradisal qualities, it was marred for me by the least heavenly animal in creation, the mosquito. Admittedly, the advent of DDT while I was there reduced its depredations and largely silenced the brain-searing whine of wings in the night that warned you, in spite of nets and 'repellant' creams, that the morning would find you bulging with hard and fiercely itching lumps, prone to turn septic in the lowland, humid heat of Colombo.

Kenya, too, has mosquitoes, but mostly, I think, in the coastal lowlands. On the savannahs of the uplands they are less troublesome. And that, for me, is one reason for making Kenya my own choice for heaven on earth, and never more so than in the early morning. For there is no sweeter air to breathe, no fairer light to see than during those hours when the sun is kindness itself to your skin. Then, nature's freer children, wise in the ways of the wild, go about their business knowing that when the sun reaches its zenith it will be time to cease to hunt or scavenge and to scurry into holes or laze in the shade of rocks or bushes.

These are the sort of 'people' I go to Kenya 'for to see' (though their human neighbours, the Masai and Samburu, are certainly worth seeing). I go there principally to see elephants making their solemn way across the open grasslands or a cheetah sitting motionless on a rock as he surveys the endless plains for a sign of breakfast. Or I might spot a lion or a leopard, still the monarchs of the wild in the average tourist's eyes and therefore supreme objectives for safari guides. Are such 'people' frightening? No, the animals rarely frighten me, but the tourists do.

There is something almost indecent about tourism. Most tourists – and I have been one many times – treat their fellow beings, animal and human, as a mere passing show. And man, being the creature he is, cannot intrude voyeuristically for long upon his fellow creatures without imposing upon them his arrogance or sentimentality; without, in fact, becoming a two-legged serpent in the unspoilt Eden.

From our vantage point in the open-topped safari bus we had spotted a circle of large-eared hunting dogs tugging at the carcase of a hare they had caught. By human standards they are not attractive animals. They are remorseless hunters with a way of life necessarily concentrated on killing. If you're a hunting dog, nobody and nothing else matters – the pack is all. Yet they, or something not unlike them, must be the progenitors of the animal that in all its forms, from the chiuhaua to the Great Dane, we worship as if we were ancient Egyptians at the feet of the dog-headed god Anubis.

Soon after seeing the pack of dogs we came upon a female leopard moving with sinuous, alert composure through the long grass, followed by three tiny cubs. We stopped the bus to watch and take photographs, while our driver-guide basked in our gratitude as the cameras clicked and a chorus of muted female 'Ahhhs' gently ruffled the morning air. Where was the beautiful rosetted cat taking her brood? Not just for a morning stroll, surely, to point out the native flora and fauna ('Now, here, dears, we have a lovely example of the African Violet, and over there I can just see a Secretary Bird').

Intent on some much more urgent purpose, she moved steadily across the grass to a hillock of outcropping stone, vanished for a moment, then emerged without her cubs. She had hidden them among the rocks, we supposed, so that she could hunt for their breakfast unimpeded.

But when the hunting dogs suddenly reappeared, she herself became the quarry. Hunters and hunted saw each other instantly and neither stopped to argue. She leapt up into a scrubby thorn tree while the dogs slavered and barked beneath her, savagely aware that they were unable to follow.

We bus-borne bipeds looked at each other, no longer mesmerised by the action, but bewildered. What, now, should we onlooking humans do? A curtain had fallen on the drama at a perfect 'cliff-hanger' moment, leaving us, the audience, as suspended, emotionally, as any treed leopard. What would happen now? Would the dogs remain – watchful, patient, menacing – at the foot of the tree while the cubs grew so hungry for their mother's milk that they forgot caution and emerged mewing from their hiding place to fall victim to some other predator? Would the dogs, as they too became famished, leave to seek an easier quarry, allowing the leopard to climb down and rejoin her cubs? In theory we were mere observers of nature. Our role was surely to go our way and 'let nature take its course'.

But it seems we never can stand back and merely watch, perhaps because we are not entirely part of nature ourselves. We are too easily swayed by notions of motherhood, fair play and the claims of the beautiful over the merely beastly – as though we had a right or even a duty to rob an animal of its hard-won dinner. Instantly the safari bus became a battle wagon fighting on behalf of the leopard. Our driver drove directly at the crowd of dogs still waiting at the foot of the tree. Hardly lowering their eyes from their intended victim in the branches, they almost casually avoided the bus. It was, at the most, a hindrance to them.

With a grinding of gears the driver changed direction to drive at them again. And after each foray they avoided the wheeled attacker, regrouping yet again at the foot of the tree. At last they seemed to recognise that the treed leopard held no future for them and took their leave unhurriedly with the safari bus close on their tails.

And that was how we left it, this 'drama of the wild' which might have been concocted for a fictionalised animal film, except that Lassie never came to the rescue. Did the leopard finally descend the tree in safety and find her cubs unharmed? Did another pack of dogs discover her or them and finish the business we had interrupted?

'Isn't nature cruel?' wailed a woman in our party.

'Of course it is, Mildred,' snapped her husband.

I think we had steak tartare for lunch when we returned to the game lodge.

23
Tomorrow?

SURROUNDED by screwed-up balls of paper I am making my fifth attempt to write a final chapter to this life-story of mine, a task which has elements in common with making a will or writing a death-bed confession. My previous efforts have degenerated into elderly moralising on the lines of 'Now, when I was a lad...' Or else they have become altogether too cosmic in tone for a book whose title indicates an emphatically regional theme.

That title, incidentally, was not chosen by me, but suggested by my publisher, who, when he invited me to write the book, endeared himself by *not* addressing me as a 'professional Yorkshireman'. That label has been hung on me more than once, as well as on better men (and possibly worse) including characters as diverse as Wilfred Pickles and J. B. Priestley. Whether it is meant as a slur or a compliment may depend on the occasion and the speaker, but it does seem to imply that one is somehow capitalising on one's origins.

And yet, why *should* being a Yorkshireman confer any automatic advantages? And are there comparable 'professional' benefits in being a Lancastrian, a Geordie or a Scot? Apparently not. Nor do we hear much about professional Londoners or Irishmen – which is not to say that there aren't any. Perhaps it is simply that Yorkshire has never lacked home-grown publicists who have convinced the world that there really is something very special indeed about being 'Yorkshire'. But that does nothing to solve the problem *why*?

Just how do you qualify as a 'professional' Tyke? By staying put, perhaps, when all about you are cutting loose, either to sail to fortune or sink without trace? Or maybe to reappear after a season to spend the rest of your life telling horror stories about what it was really like in the big, wide, wicked world beyond the Ridings? Or does it mean staying put in a spiritual sense, as perhaps Priestley did, despite his wanderings. For most of my life I have stayed put in a physical sense and have many times been asked why. Due to the mystique of what used to be known as Fleet Street, that question is more often put to journalists than to doctors, schoolmasters or estate agents; but my only answer must be that I saw no good and sufficient reason to leave.

Perhaps my fate was sealed one day when, having survived our daily stint on the *Yorkshire Evening News* sub-editors' 'table', my colleague Jack Child and I awaited our homeward bus in Leeds. Jack took from his pocket a copy of *World's Press News*, or perhaps it was *Newspaper World*, and scanned the 'Jobs' page. 'Mmh . . . *Yorkshire Life*. Just suit you, that one,' he mused and, without knowing it, he pointed his finger at my future.

I knew he was right. After about seven years in the comparatively hectic world of evening papers, the prospect of editing a monthly magazine like *Yorkshire Life Illustrated* (as it was called then) had enormous appeal; not just because it seemed to promise a less stressful existence (which proved to be not always the case), but because it also offered me a chance to *write*.

Such chances were not too plentiful. True enough, I had somehow, during my newspaper days, persuaded the features editor of the *Yorkshire Evening News* to publish one or two short stories. But the editor himself, the legendary R. W. Shawcross, seemed to take a rather discouraging view of scribbling sub-editors, in case they provoked rumbles of discontent from the reporters' room. I could have asked for a transfer to Features, but sub-editors were so chronically in short supply that it would hardly have been granted. So the magazine field had its attractions.

Certainly my writing apprenticeship began in earnest when I joined *Yorkshire Life*. How far I completed that apprenticeship is for the reader to judge, but whether I did or not, I certainly learned a great deal about Yorkshire and the magnificence of a countryside I had till then only glimpsed in well-trodden tourist haunts. And, since the truly great county of my birth is a microcosm of England, and perhaps even of 'the great globe itself', I learned about much besides writing.

Yorkshire, I was discovering, 'had everything', and that everything was open to me to explore. I could lunch with an archbishop in York or with the down-and-outs at St George's Crypt in Leeds. I could commission articles on whatever subject took my fancy, rashly confident that it would also take the fancy of my readers. I could explore varied industries as well as spacious moors and dales and a colourful and historic coastline, make friends with poets and artists, librarians and eccentrics, take visiting actresses to lunch and live, in short, the life of Riley, had he but been a Yorkshireman.

There were occasions when, as opportunity arose, I even showed the Yorkshire flag as far afield as Israel or Hungary. And, 'in and among' all this, as my late lamented chief sub Bill Lowis might have said, I began writing books. I was in fact encouraged to do so by my own employers, the Whitethorn Press (as they were then), who published three of them, the first being *Queer Folk*, sub-titled 'A Yorkshire Comicality' (which seemed more inviting than 'A Collection of Yorkshire Oddballs'). The writing of this epic was not entirely an altruistic attempt to boost my employer's profits. It seemed politic, however, in view of the fact that I planned to write more books, to offer one or two to the people who paid my salary.

Queer Folk, in spite of the misgivings of one director, who failed to see why anybody should be 'interested in eccentrics', instantly took off. If it were true that nobody cared for oddballs, that fact was certainly unknown to the *Daily Mail*, which gave generous coverage to the book – though their own interest was more than likely inspired by the sort of playful trans-Pennine bias you might expect from a northern edition emanating from Manchester. We always knew, said their writer, in effect, that Yorkshiremen were crackpots. Now here's a book that proves it.

There was obviously no such bias on the part of Yorkshire Television who, before interviewing me 'live' as the author of *Queer Folk*, imaginatively up-dated the antics of my subjects and presented them as spoofy news items of the present day. They included Bill Sharp, who went to bed for fifty years when his beloved left him waiting at the church; Jemmy Hirst, whose vagaries won him an audience with George III; Charles Waterton, who captured an alligator by riding on its back, and Job Senior, who gave advice to the lovelorn from his dog kennel of a home on Ilkley Moor.

In the intervals of trying to prove my unwavering belief that a Yorkshire magazine need not lack excellence through being home-grown, I have written other books, culminating in this one, the most challenging, yet the most satisfying of them all. I still haven't quite recovered from the surprise of being asked to do it, because somehow it had never struck me that there was anything particularly unusual about my own 'Yorkshire life' and the way I had spent it.

Others have been less blasé about it. How, they have sometimes asked me, could I possibly have spent more than thirty years in the same job without dying of boredom? I began to feel like one of my own 'queer folk', but could only reply that my life has been, and remains, singularly happy and that I have never been bored with any part of it; certainly not since my teenage years, though I was restless enough then at times.

Writing your memoirs reminds you more forcibly even than the making of your will that you are mortal. Like an impending execution, which indeed it is, your eventual demise must concentrate the mind most wonderfully, and there is no doubt that it gives one furiously to think. Yet from the moment a reputable publisher, apparently sober and in his right mind, says, 'Have you ever thought of writing your life?' that life takes on a new significance.

'Who, me?' you feel like saying, uneasily conscious that in your youth the cardinal sin was to 'think you were somebody'. At the same time, you were expected in those days to believe that *everybody* was somebody. Not a sparrow fell but God was mindful of it, and we, as human beings, never questioned that we were worth more than many sparrows. But that of course was before the days when some so-called animal-lovers could express their concern for sparrows and the like by poisoning the food of human babies.

We believed that man had a goal and a soul. It mattered *how* you lived your life, and mattered a great deal more than what might happen to you here on earth, because everything would be sorted out in terms of your eternal felicity, or otherwise, when you reached what my grandmother-in-law used to call 'the Farther Shore'. She sang hymns about what would happen when we 'gathered at the river' and had little doubt that for her, at least, the eternal future would be bright.

We were less confident about the sheep in other folds; Anglicans would have to make out a pretty strong case to make up for their laxity over things like raffle tickets and alcoholic communion wine and their reliance on ceremonies like confirmation. As for the RCs, they were on a hiding to nothing. One way and another, for the believing Nonconformist of my childhood days, the next world was very nearly as real as this. I can remember a discussion. probably between a Christadelphian aunt and her Independent Methodist brothers-in-law, as to whether redeemed parents in the hereafter might have the doubtful privilege of witnessing the eternal sufferings down below of their no-good offspring. The consensus was that this would add nothing to their felicity (contrary, by the way, to the reported opinion of some of the early fathers of the Church).

But by the time I was old enough to listen to what the preacher was saying, hell was on its last legs, so to speak – the old hell, that is, of fire and brimstone – but it was not quite dead. Nor was the day of pulpit histrionics. It was not at all unusual for one preacher to burst into song and expect the congregation to join him. First he told you what a sinner he used to be – 'there was drinking, friends; there was smoking, there was women'. (Our adolescent ears pricked up, for pulpit revelations usually skirted – no pun intended – over that one.) Then he would sing with increasing fervour, 'Spirit of the living God, fall afresh on me,' the organist obligingly joining in as soon as he had got the hang of the tune.

Nor did it always stop at impromptu solos. There was, for instance, the legendary preacher who would demonstrate most graphically the effects of sin. 'Dear friends,' he would warn, 'a man goes down to hell like this' (whereupon he would slide down the rail of the pulpit steps) 'but he climbs out of the pit like this –' illustrating the laborious return to righteousness as he struggled back up the steps.

There were saints among these zealots, just as there were bores and – humanity being what it is – occasional hypocrites. There were also would-be intellectuals who larded their discourse with mispronounced words picked up during solemn and studious hours spent poring over books from the Theology section of the local library: a favourite example from my own collection was 'chaosness', the 'ch' being pronounced as in 'China'.

They were not by any means all Bible-bashing bigots. Compared with the mass of their more orthodox contemporaries, many were earnest, deep-thinking, self-educated men, diligent in their search for truth and often decidedly liberal in their views. Dad certainly was: during an after-chapel discussion on hell, he casually but confidently disposed of eternal punishment by pronouncing, 'There *isn't* any hell!' Mother gave him the sort of look some wives might have thrown him for admiring another woman. 'It's t' first time *I* knew you didn't believe in hell,' she accused. Could this really be the man she had married?

Nowadays, people do not seem to know what they believe, only what they don't believe. Yet the amount of sincere voluntary service performed by many for their fellow humans strikes me as amazing. And for non-humans, too, though it is a pity that this laudable concern for 'minorities' seems to topple over at times into the hatred by a lunatic fringe for the more conformist majority. Perhaps in due course a balance will be restored and the religion of the future will concern itself with the sacredness of the earth and of life in all its forms.

Indeed, to me, life is the everlasting mystery, whether this homely Yorkshire life of mine or the life which insists, both in microbe and man, on asserting its claim to existence; adapting itself to what might seem the most inhospitable conditions, here on earth and perhaps, in one form or another, throughout the universe. Is there purpose in life? If not, why do all life's creatures struggle so painfully to survive and to hand on the gift of life to their young?

This life of mine, I feel, could hardly have been spent in a period of greater change – though who knows what changes lie ahead? In Yorkshire, great industries like coal and steel and fishing have dwindled almost before the disbelieving eyes of the men who were proud to serve them, leaving only bitterness and despair. On a more trivial level, bureaucrats, through ignorance, one hopes, rather than malice, have robbed us of our Ridings, symbols of a thousand years of history.

As I approach the end of my journey I realise more and more that if ever I have been less than happy, it has probably been my own fault. So many people have shown me far more kindness than I deserved: my parents, whom I increasingly recognise, as the years go by, as a most remarkable pair; my wife, who must surely be the only woman who could tolerate me, and my children who have brought me joy and pride.

What lies ahead as I approach the 'Farther Shore' so confidently anticipated by my grandmother-in-law? Perhaps not the pearly gates she looked for, but at worst, perhaps, the good sleep which Marcus Aurelius saw as nothing to dread. But there may also be those revelations, reported down the centuries and now eagerly studied as 'near-death experiences', which have opened 'windows on eternity' for resuscitated accident victims and others.

Life remains a fascinating mystery, and so is its ending. Remarkable men have remarkable views on death, which they are able to view with equanimity and even excitement. Group Captain Leonard Cheshire, war hero and friend to the disabled, saw it as 'the culmination of life'; Chad Varah, founder of the Samaritans and an Anglican priest, seems convinced of the truth of reincarnation. He may be right, in which case, perhaps there is yet another 'Yorkshire life' in store for me. Or maybe I'll return as an African Hottentot or even a Lancastrian! In any case, we are children of life and must do as she tells us, trusting, with those like Juliana of Norwich, who can maybe see a little farther, that 'all shall be well'.